Brandon Roy

Guy Mervyn

Vol. II

Brandon Roy

Guy Mervyn
Vol. II

ISBN/EAN: 9783337039929

Printed in Europe, USA, Canada, Australia, Japan

Cover: Foto ©ninafisch / pixelio.de

More available books at **www.hansebooks.com**

A Novel

BY

BRANDON ROY

IN THREE VOLUMES
VOL. II.

LONDON
SPENCER BLACKETT
35, ST. BRIDE STREET, LUDGATE CIRCUS, E.C.
1891

GUY MERVYN.

CHAPTER XV.

"Cyril, there is one thing I cannot understand about you."

"And what is that, Guy?"

It was the evening of the day Guy had received Beryl's letter. The two young men were strolling about in the moonlight; enjoying the cool evening breeze, and watching the wonderful Diablerets glacier, brilliantly lit up by the moonbeams. Guy hesitated, then said, suddenly:

"You are so hard on the girl you love."

Cyril Branscome winced, and a dark look

passed over his face, but vanished almost instantly.

"In what way?" he asked quietly, but in a tone of suppressed annoyance.

Guy heard it, and knew he was on dangerous ground; but the mournful questioning look in those sweet brown eyes rose before him, as it had done many times since that evening at Vevey; and he steeled himself to say this which had so long been on his mind, even at the risk of offending his friend.

"I don't want to vex you, old fellow," he said, "and you must forgive me, if I speak too bluntly; but it seems to me that you treat her as you would treat no one else in this world."

"I *love* her as I love no one else in this world," said Cyril bitterly.

"But that fact should tell just the other way," answered Guy. "You do not naturally judge people harshly. I have often noticed how ready you are to see the best side of anyone, and to put the kindest and most charitable construction on their actions. But for *her* there is to be no quarter, no excuse. Because she has failed you once, therefore she is to be deemed fickle and false for ever. Cyril, it is hard on her, cruelly hard!"

Cyril laughed, but the pain in his laugh was terrible to hear.

"My dear boy," he said, "what do you know of love—such love as mine for her? You talk as though a man could be refused once a week by the girl he loves. No, Mervyn. A man who possesses any manly self-respect puts that question *once*, and takes his answer; but, be it for weal or woe, he abides by it, and never asks it again. If a girl intends to refuse him the first time, she would refuse him the second; if she is so wantonly heartless and flippant as to say *no*, when she really means *yes*, just to test her power over him, or to see what anguish one little word of two letters from her lips can cause; why, then, she is not worthy a true man's love, and he is well out of it, say I! No, I would never put that question twice."

"I would," said Guy, "ay, or a hundred times; and take a *no* for ninety-nine, if she gave me her love and her heart at the hundredth time of asking!"

"Wait till you have tried it *once*," said Cyril. "And now let us change the subject; it is not a very pleasant one."

"In a moment," said Guy. "For the sake of our strong friendship, Cyril, let me say one thing more; and then, if you wish, drop it for ever."

"Well, say on."

"Cyril, I honestly believe that girl loves you now; and more unselfishly and truly than you love her. I never shall forget the look of pain and anguish in her eyes, when you left the table that night; such an expression of sorrow, and bitter grief, I never saw in human eyes before. She may have been influenced against you once ; but, believe me, she loves you now."

Guy paused. Cyril Branscome made no reply. His half-averted face seemed to say : " Have you done ?"

" How easily a misunderstanding may have arisen under those strange circumstances of which you told me ; she may have been compelled by her father to refuse you, while all the time her heart was yours. If so, what needless misery you are both suffering. Why not write and ask her if she really meant what she said that night ? Could you not forgive her, if she had weakly yielded to a stronger will ? Could you not be as generous and kind to *her* as you would be to any other friend who had wronged you ?"

Cyril stopped, and sat down on the mossy trunk of a fallen tree. Guy leaned his back against one opposite, and for a time both were silent. When at last Cyril spoke, all trace of vexation had passed out of his voice.

"Guy," he said, with a sad smile, "you know so little of the ways of women. You judge them generously, frankly, kindly, according to the impulse of your own warm heart; but you have never yet been wronged by one; God grant you never may be. You have never had your life blighted at its brightest moment, your hopes shattered on the eve of fulfilment. I know you have spoken out of true friendship for me; I don't misunderstand you; but let us mention the subject no more. It had best remain dead and buried. I have often thought of the possibilities you suggest, but none of them hold good. She knew my address and could have easily communicated with me at the time, if she had been in any way coerced by her father; besides, this much I will tell you, Guy; I did write her one desperate letter, reminding her of our love, and imploring her to reconsider her decision, and——"

"And what?" cried Guy eagerly.

"I got no answer."

"Cyril," said Guy, "can you forgive me for plaguing you with my idiotic talk? I was a confounded fool to suppose I could judge in such a matter! But I hope to goodness, old fellow, you will some day find a true-hearted girl worthy of you, and be happy ever after."

Cyril smiled sadly, and shook his head; then lighted a cigarette and smoked in silence. Guy, still leaning his back against a tree, softly hummed to himself:

"And for bonnie Annie Laurie
I'd lay me doon and dee."

Suddenly he stopped, and turning to his friend, said abruptly:

"Cyril, do you believe in the Bible?"

"A queer question to ask a clergyman, my dear fellow," Cyril Branscome answered, rather sarcastically.

"Yes, but *do* you?"

"Well, yes, I suppose I do."

"What do you believe about it?"

"Well, I believe it is true."

"Every word?"

"I suppose so."

"True now, or true when it was written?"

"Well, both, I should think. But what are you driving at?"

Guy did not answer for a minute. Then he said, speaking rather hurriedly: "I think the moonlight makes one talk. Any way I feel inclined to, to-night; and I want to tell you something which has been much on my mind lately. Do you remember that evening in London, the day before we crossed to France, when you were busy settling everything, and getting together all we wanted?"

"And you could settle to nothing, and went off at last for two or three hours, leaving me to arrange things as best I could? Of course I do."

"Well, I was awfully wretched that day.

You know why, now. I felt almost mad with love and despair, and the thought that if I had not been such a mad fool I might have been meeting her every day, instead of having to go off, and perhaps never see her again ; and it was so terrible to know that if ever she thought of me now, it would be with feelings of scorn and dislike. I am afraid I led you rather a life in those first days; but, as I say, I felt hopeless, reckless, mad. Well, when I went off that night, it was to a concert. I happened to take up a paper, and saw it announced ; and what specially caught my eye was this : *Solo violin, Madame Norman - Neruda.* Now don't begin to argue, Cyril ; I won't be interrupted ! You know nothing about violins or violin playing, and I do ; and I tell you again, she is the queen of violinists ! There is something about her playing which moves one, as no other can ever do. Well, when I got to the Hall, the concert had begun.

There happened to be one vacant seat in the stalls. I paid for it, and went in. Someone was singing, I have not a notion who, or what; but it was a love song, and I wished I hadn't come; and should have got up and left, only I thought it would seem rather queer to go out at once, after paying a guinea to go in. Well, the song came to an end at last, and so did two or three others; then there was a pause; a fellow came up and struck a chord on the piano; a faint answering echo sounded from a violin; then Madame Neruda came on, to play. Cyril, never to my dying day shall I forget the sound of that violin! Two pieces were down on the programme, to follow one another. The first was a weird fantastic scherzo. She played it—ah! she *did* play it! You might almost have thought that violin was possessed by something supernatural! And the whole thing seemed to me an exact setting to music of the reckless, passionate, desperate misery raging in my own heart. I had an answering echo for every note; and when at last it ceased with a mad, wild chord — an end without an ending — I felt that my own wretchedness would go on like that for ever, and have no end. There was a pause. Madame Neruda looked quietly round for one moment. Then she raised her bow, and a low sad minor theme came slowly wailing forth. Oh, the depth, the tenderness, the pathos of those notes, pass all power of description. I sat spellbound. The audience, the concert hall, everything, vanished. I seemed alone with that violin, as it sighed out a sorrow sad and deep as my own. All the passion was gone, all the recklessness was over; and it died out of my heart, too; and these sad minor notes took its place. But suddenly they rose and fell, clearer, louder, brighter; then passed into the major key, and burst into a glorious song of triumphant praise; settling at last into quiet sweeping notes of rest and peace.

"It was over. The audience applauding loudly, brought one back to the realities of life; especially as an old gentleman sitting next me thumped violently on my toe with his cane. Madame Neruda gracefully acknowledged the thunders of applause, and left the platform; and though recalled enthusiastically, did not play again. Then I got up and went out. Cyril, for days that music haunted me; it haunts me still. This thought was constantly in my mind. May not my sorrow also end in joy? Is there not peace, deep peace, somewhere for my restless unsatisfied heart, if only I knew where to find it? Perhaps, to you, it will seem absurd that violin playing should so have affected my mind, and dwelt in my thoughts; but if you loved music as I do, you would understand it.

"Well, you remember I told you about *her*

telling me, half in play, all sorts of things I ought to do to improve myself? One was to read the Bible. I did not think of it again at the time, but just before we left home her own little Bible came into my possession; and afterwards, in thinking over all she had ever said to me, I remembered that, and it seemed a sort of sad pleasure to do every little thing she had told me to do, although she would never know it. So the very night we came away I read a chapter out of her Bible; and I have never failed to do so since, though I believe that was the first time in my life I ever read a chapter through of my own accord. But I thought it precious dull work, except for its being out of her book, and a sort of link between her and me. But the night after the concert I came on something that startled me. That violin still sounded in my ears; and when I was alone that night the thought came up again strongly in my mind: May not my trouble also end in triumph? Is there not peace somewhere to be found, if only I knew where to find it? I opened her little Bible, hardly thinking of what I was doing, and the first thing I read was this: '*The peace of God passeth all understanding.*' Cyril, what is the peace of God?"

Cyril Branscome flung away his cigarette, got up, and stood with his hand on the tree against which Guy was leaning. His face looked white in the moonlight.

"Guy," he said in a low tone, "it is no good asking me about these sort of things, because I know no more about them than you do."

"But you are a parson," objected Guy.

"I know it," answered Cyril bitterly. "But why did I take orders? Only because that was the most speedy way of obtaining the wish of my life; and when I lost my love, I lost what little faith, and hope, and peace I did possess. I can tell you of doctrine, all you wish; but, Guy, you are seeking after *realities*, and there I cannot help you."

"Then you believe there are realities in all this, if only we could find them?" asked Guy eagerly.

"I don't know what to believe," said Cyril moodily. "Nothing is real to me."

He turned away, and walked silently back through the wood. Guy followed, and neither spoke again until they reached their rooms. Cyril paused at the door of his.

"Good-night, old fellow," he said.

But Guy came in, and lingered, talking lightly of many things. At last he said, with an effort:

"Don't let us drop that subject now we have once started it. I've been wanting to bring it up for days; but somehow it was not easy to begin."

"But talking to me won't help you," said Cyril gloomily.

"Yes, it will," said Guy, "because there is

no cant, and no sham, and no humbug about you."

"And no reality either," put in Cyril.

"Nonsense!" said Guy. "You're down in the mouth to-night. But look here! I have always thought religion was more or less of humbug; all very well for priests and old women, but not the sort of thing for fellows like you and me. I knew I was bound to go to hell some day, but then that was settled long before I was born; and 'what can't be cured must be endured' is a favourite motto of mine. Well, then, of course I had heard of the atonement made by the death of Christ, and how, through Him, a certain chosen few, who went through some mysterious process by faith, could be 'brought nigh' and reconciled to God. But that was the very last thing I wanted. God was going to damn the world, and do the same to me, unless I turned very religious, and went through this process of reconciliation, through the intercession of the Saviour; and—I hope it is not very profane to say so—but really, Cyril, I had no wish at all to be brought nigh to such a God as that—angry, and for ever judging, banishing, and condemning. Not that I ever thought much about it; but when I did think, it was rather indefinitely in that sort of way. So I made up my mind to get as much pleasure and enjoyment out of life as possible; and afterwards—if there were such a place as hell—why, make the best of it when I got there. But now——"

Guy paused.

"Well," asked Cyril, "what now?"

"Now all looks so different. To begin with, when I took to reading the Bible for myself, I found I'd been taught all wrong from beginning to end. There is precious little in it, that I can see, about hell-fire, or about a 'chosen few'; but a vast amount about a grand free pardon for all the world, if they will have it. And then I looked for the wrath, and anger, and everlasting vengeance; but instead *love*—love was everywhere; it seemed to shine out of every page. This puzzled me tremendously. At last, one night, I said to myself: Yes, I *do* believe in the love of Jesus. Who could have done more to prove love than He did ? What's more, I do believe *He* would make things all square even for *me*, if He could ; but how about *God?* And I began to think over all I had ever heard about an avenging God, and a righteous Judge, banishing and damning all who were not as righteous as He ; and I thought of so many awful things, that the love of Christ, in which I was just beginning to believe, was thrown into the shade ; the love which saved the few, seemed as nothing to the awful wrath which damned the many. Cyril, I felt a sort of hopeless horror, and wished I had never thought at all about the subject. To put it out of my head, I turned to look out a few more loving tender words of His; and almost the first I came on were these: '*The Father Himself loveth you.*' Then there flashed into my mind a text I had learnt years ago, and often repeated without a thought as to its meaning: '*God so loved* the world that *He gave* His only begotten Son, that whosoever believeth in Him should not perish, but have everlasting life.' Why—I thought—surely the *sending* was harder than the *going;* and the love that *gave* as great, or greater, than the love that *went?* And oh, Cyril!" Guy's earnest young voice trembled with strong emotion, as he spoke: "Oh, Cyril, I did feel such an ungrateful brute, when I remembered all I had been thinking just before. It seemed as bad as if I had wronged and misjudged my mother. Then I thought, but *she* would know of it, and He does not. And instantly came the answer, clear and quick, as though it had been spoken: 'He *does.*' And I looked up, and said right out loud: 'But He doesn't *care*,' and back came that quiet answer: 'He *does*.' Do you know, I felt so bad, that, almost before I knew what I was about, I had blown out the candle and jumped into bed, and pulled all the clothes over my head, as I used to do long ago when I was a little chap, and had vexed my mother."

Half ashamed of that tiresome quiver in his voice, which would not be controlled, Guy paused and looked shyly at his friend.

But he had no need to fear chaff from Cyril Branscome. He stood leaning against the window-frame, in the same attitude as on that last night at Vevey when Guy found him in his room, after the chance meeting with his lost sweetheart, his forehead pressed hard against the cool pane of glass. He did not speak; and Guy, having once stopped, found it difficult to begin again. So they stood together silently, looking out upon the perfect stillness of the moonlit scene before them; every tree and twig showing clear in the calm silvery light; not a leaf stirring, not a blade of grass moving; all nature seemed bewitched by that great bright moon, sailing majestically overhead. The silence would have been as complete as the stillness, had it not been for the ceaseless roar of the mountain torrent, as it rushed past, on its downward way to the valley.

And Cyril, as he stands there, feels that but for that wild rushing sound, he must burst into harsh, discordant laughter, just to mar the peace and stillness around him. A silent surging torrent of terrible thoughts is passing through his mind. All the awful doubts, the subtle insinuations, the convincing arguments, the countless speculations and theories which have long since robbed him of every shred of simple faith, now chase one another in rapid succession through his brain. An impulse, which he knows to be fiendish, but which nevertheless seems irresistible, moves him to turn, and speak them all out; and thus, with one breath, blast for ever these young tendrils of faith and hope, just beginning to spring up in his friend's heart, and feel about for the Rock of Ages, if haply they may find It and cling to It, and grow there in safety. One word from him, and Guy's face will never wear again that earnest, half-hopeful, upward look. One unanswerable theory put forward and all these new thoughts and dreams will be dispelled, and vanish, once and forever.

So thought Cyril, remembering how quickly his own faith—which had never been real faith—had left him; and how easily his peace—which was such as the world giveth—had been destroyed. So thought Cyril, not knowing that it is written: "If it be of God, ye cannot overthrow it."

Twice he turned to his companion, as if about to speak; and twice turned back again, and looked out into the moonlight. Then he said in a low voice, without looking at Guy:

" Well, what more ?"

" I scarcely know," said Guy, thankful to have the silence broken, and be launched again. " I can't explain it or express it, but somehow I feel in a kind of maze; which I never meant to enter, and out of which I cannot find my way. The clue to the whole thing—the one question on which it seems to hinge—is this: Are all these things *realities*, such realities as can affect a fellow's life; or are they only stories—fables about dead and gone things, which did—or didn't—happen, in a far-away past? It is one thing to read of a Saviour having died for the world eighteen hundred years and more before we were born or thought of; and quite another to know that now, at this very moment, *I* have a Saviour, whom I do not care for, do not love, do not think of; whose existence makes no difference in my life; yet who is watching me, caring for me, planning for me, and above all, loving me with unutterable love; such love, that it makes a fellow feel awfully mean, to go on living without a thought for Him. I tell you, Cyril—if I believed in Him—I'd live for Him! I'd give up going on in my own ways, and find out His. Not that there would be any merit in that, for I'm precious sick of my own ways, and all connected with them. I used to think this world jolly all round, and everything I wanted; but now that I have had my first trouble, all looks so different. One can't be sure of anyone or anything here; I want someone I *can* be sure of; someone I can trust and depend upon; someone stronger than myself. Did you not feel so, when you had your disappointment?"

Cyril did not answer.

"Well," said Guy, stretching himself and squaring his shoulders, " no doubt you think me a sentimental fool; and so I have called myself over and over. But mind, Cyril, it is not *religion*. Don't think I am going to turn religious. Not I! It is not a lot of canting humbug I want, but downright realities; not a lot of theories, but a living Person. And, do you know, I saw last night that it does say: 'They that seek Me, *shall* find Me.'"

"And—have you—sought Him?"

Cyril turned as he put the question; but a cloud just then obscured the moon, and neither could see the other's face.

"No," replied Guy solemnly, speaking very low. "It seems such a test, Cyril. Somehow either way I should dread the result. If it were true, and I found Him, it would be so—so awfully wonderful; but suppose I did not find Him, then all would be over; it would not be true; there would be no more hope."

"It *is* a test," said Cyril; "and, in these cases, tests generally prove——"

"What?" inquired Guy eagerly.

"Oh, no matter," said Cyril, rather wearily, turning away again. "I told you it was no good asking *me* about such things."

"Well, good-night, old fellow. I shall be up at sunrise to-morrow, and off to find the edelweiss long before you're awake, unless you will change your mind and come. No? All right, then; don't wait breakfast or lunch. Old Mother Dubuis will pack enough for both into my knapsack. Expect me when you see me; and if I fall over a precipice, break the news gently to my mother and Beryl; but quote Mephistopheles to Gertrude, thus: 'Madam, your brother's dead, and sends his love.'"

Cyril smiled.

"Take care of yourself, Guy, for my sake. They would never forgive me if anything went wrong. Good-night."

"Good-night."

Guy went whistling down the passage, and Cyril heard his door bang noisily.

Cyril Branscome still stood musing at the window. "Poor boy!" he murmured to himself; "he half believes already; but knows enough to fear a test. No wonder; well he may. Which of my beliefs for one moment stood a test? Not one." Then involuntarily he started, as Guy's words returned to his mind: "I want downright realities, not a lot of theories;" followed, like a lightning flash, by the question: "Have I ever known realities; or has it been with me, always only theories?"

And the answer would not be stifled, but came back at once, though soft and low, at first, as a mental echo: "always only theories—only theories."

Then Cyril Branscome struck a light, got out his best theological books, and settled down to study. He sat at the little rough deal table in his room, with his back to the window; though he had already drawn the curtain to shut out that 'witching moonlit scene. His elbows resting on the table, his head in his hands, his book before him; he was ready for stern thought, and deep study. He would banish these strange, sweet, mystic thoughts from his mind, as easily as he had shut out the moonlight.

Perfect silence reigned around, unbroken save by the distant rushing of the torrent. Even Guy's whistling, which had come to him half muffled through the intervening doors for the last ten minutes, had ceased now; and all was still. No one was up in the whole house but himself. What a grand opportunity for reading hard.

But why would that mountain stream, as it dashed along, keep on repeating: *Always only theories—only theories?* What a first-class theologian he had been at college—*always only theories!* Surely he ought to know all that could be known upon these subjects, seeing they were the very ones in which he had taken the highest honours--

always only theories! This very book before him was the one he had then found most useful in his work. It contained all that the wisdom of the wisest could write, on even the most doubtful points—*always only theories—only theories!*

Cyril Branscome rose, put away his divinity books, and drew from the place where he kept them under lock and key, the last volumes he had purchased of sceptical writings. The book he first opened, and tried to read, was one which he firmly believed contained that which must effectually and entirely upset all faith in the old-fashioned ideas and beliefs of his childhood and youth. He was anxious entirely to master its contents to-night; and then, if Guy began this sort of talk again, well then, perhaps——

But now the torrent also changed its theme, and ceaselessly rose and fell, murmuring: *No realities, no realities.*

Cyril flung away his book, with a gesture of impatience. "What has come to me?" he cried half angrily; "why on earth can't I read in peace to-night? The room is stiflingly hot." He rose hastily, tore aside the curtain, and threw open the window. Still that same calm, quiet moonlight; but a cool night breeze had risen, and gently fanned his hot forehead. The stillness was oppressive. If only he could hear Guy's cheery "Hullo there!" from that quiet wood beyond; or his merry whistle along the passage! Moved by a sudden impulse to escape somehow from this perfect solitude, he took up his candle, and went to Guy's room.

He opened the door noiselessly, and entered. Guy was sound asleep, as he expected. Shading the light with one hand, Cyril gently crossed the little room, and stood looking at his friend.

Guy lay in a deep restful slumber, one arm thrown above his head, the other stretched towards the table near his bedside, as if his last thoughts had been of something there. His brown wavy hair, allowed to grow to what he laughingly called a "musical length," now fell lightly across his forehead; his face, half turned towards Cyril, wore a wonderfully peaceful, happy expression.

"I don't believe that fellow has ever done a really wrong thing in his life," mused Cyril to himself. "This escapade, over which he is so heartbroken, and which is evidently his worst, most young men of his age would consider a mere joke. Yet Guy thinks he has outraged the sex, and broken all the laws of chivalry and manhood! I wonder what he would say of some fellows and their doings. What a fine study he would make for a picture of young Sir Galahad seeking the holy Grail! Ah!—*seeking*——"

The word recalled to his mind their conversation, and his interrupted train of thought.

He glanced at the table near which Guy's hand rested. Close to the extinguished light lay a small book bound in purple morocco. Cyril knew it in a moment to be the book which had started such strange new ideas in Guy's mind. He set down his candle, took it up, and turned over the pages. But as he did so, the fly-leaf caught his eye, and he read the one word—*Elaine.* So that was her name—the only thing in the whole story which Guy had kept back from him. Cyril hastily put down the book, feeling that by this discovery, all unintentional though it was, he had wronged his sleeping friend. With one backward glance at Guy, he returned to his room; but not to rest. Sleep seemed to have left him to-night. He searched among his books for his own Bible, and found it at last in a forgotten corner at the bottom of the box. Then he lighted a fresh candle, and sat down for the third time to study: to look out these passages which had so struck Guy, and fathom their full meaning.

Daylight dawned and crept in through the half-closed curtain. Cyril still sat at his table, his head in his hands, wrapt in deep thought.

The candle flickered in the socket, and went out. Its last expiring efforts to keep alight aroused Cyril, and looking up, he saw that it was broad daylight. At the same moment a queer, shuffling step passed down the passage, followed by a low knocking at a door, and a sepulchral stagey whisper. It was good old Madame Dubuis calling Guy at sunrise, according to promise. Cyril only waited to hear Guy's loud "All right"; then, conscious of nothing but a splitting headache, he threw himself on his bed, and was soon asleep.

※　　※　　※　　※　　※

And Guy?

Guy went out briskly into the fresh morning air, and started on his long mountain climb. All nature awoke as he passed on his way. The lark rose up from the grass at his feet, and soared into the sky.

His mind was full of wonderful new thoughts. Day was also dawning there, and a little lark in his heart was waking into life, and soaring upwards.

Guy was seeking. For the edelweiss? Maybe.

Up, up, he went; and found the bright blue gentian — emblem of hope. Higher still, and he found the rare edelweiss — emblem of a life of stainless purity. Higher — still higher — and he found — ah! who shall say what he found; for "it passeth knowledge": and those who would know it must also seek and find it for themselves.

* * * * *

Cyril Branscome began to grow anxious. Evening was drawing near, and Guy had not returned. Old Madame Dubuis had come out many times, shading her eyes with her hand, and looked up at the glacier; not that she could have seen Guy at that distance, even had he been there.

At length Cyril heard him whistling through the wood, and went to meet him.

They met close to the fallen tree where they had talked the night before.

"Well, you are a nice fellow to have charge of!" cried Cyril, as Guy came in sight. "You call this being back to lunch! Here is old Mother Dubuis breaking her heart lest you—Hullo! What's up?"

Something undefinable in Guy's face made him stop short and put the question.

Guy took him by both hands.

"Cyril," he said, with a thrill of deep feeling in his voice, "Cyril, old fellow, I've found it!"

"Found what, Guy?"

"I've found the peace of God, which passeth all understanding. I've found the living, loving Saviour I was seeking. Cyril—He gave Himself for me, and I have given myself to Him, this day."

CHAPTER XVI.

THE month of June had come round again, and an unusually warm and lovely June it was. The woods around Mervyn Hall wore their freshest, brightest attire; and on this particular day were so gay with flowers, and so overflowing with the joyous songs of birds, that, as Lady Elaine passed through them, they seemed an enchanted land of loveliness.

Lady Elaine had been calling at Mervyn Hall, and was now returning on foot to The Towers, by the short way through the woods. She was thinking, as she went, of how, a year ago almost to the very day, she had done exactly the same thing. History often repeats itself in this everyday life of ours. Having heard of Mrs. Mervyn's return to the Hall, she had ordered her carriage at three, and driven over there. Just as before, she had seen Mrs. Mervyn and the two girls, and sat through a rather tedious twenty minutes in the drawing-room; only, this time she really tried to be friendly and cordial, and met with rather a chilly reception. Then, tempted as before, by the beauty of the afternoon, she had sent her carriage home, and was now walking slowly back through the woods. The only difference between what occurred this year and last, being that neither Bidger nor his master appeared upon the scene.

Guy was still abroad, Mrs. Mervyn had said; but she did not volunteer any information as to when they expected him home; and though Lady Elaine wished to know, she did not ask. The Mervyns were not very communicative during her visit; but this much she learned, chiefly from Beryl, that they had joined Guy and Mr. Branscome at Cannes, in October, where they spent the whole winter; that Guy had travelled about most of the time, and had been to Spain and Italy; that when they left Cannes, early in May, Guy took them to see a favourite little place of his in Switzerland, which was very beautiful, but being high up in the mountains rather too cold after Cannes; that they were very pleased to get back and find England looking so lovely; and Guy? Oh, Guy was still abroad.

Lady Elaine walked on until she reached the very spot where Bidger so unceremoniously jumped out upon her. Then she stopped, and sat down on the soft moss to rest—and think.

Why had not Guy Mervyn come home? Could what happened the last time they were in these woods together be still keeping him away? Surely he must know that by now she would have forgotten as well as forgiven it. She thought over every detail of that scene ; it all came back vividly to her mind, as it had often done since. Lady Elaine, in common with most of her sex, was rather illogical ; and, though she expected Guy to know she had forgotten it, she did not consider that in the least incompatible with preserving an accurate recollection of every particular.

And after all, it looked very different at this distance of time. She had been much too hard on Guy, who was only an enthusiastic boy, and should have been treated as such. And then—all said and done—it is very sweet to be loved, especially when one's life is lonely and loveless. And if she had kept him beside her, instead of driving him away, might she not have turned his feeling for her to good account, by using all her influence with him rightly and well? If so, she had certainly lost an opportunity for good by treating his boyish enthusiasm, and momentary loss of self-control, as an unpardonable offence. No doubt, by now, he had forgotten her, amongst those many new interests and varied scenes. Well, no matter now; but still, all said and done, it is so sweet to be loved. Sitting there, just where he overtook her a year ago, her mind naturally went back to their first meeting. She saw him, as she had seen him then, standing before her, cap in hand; the sunbeams shining through the trees upon his head; that half penitent, half comical expression in his blue eyes, as he looked down at her wistfully, saying: "You know, I'm awfully sorry." She smiled in spite of herself at the recollection; then sighed, and said: "I wish he would come back." He had come into her life, just as a gleam of brilliant sunshine bursts out between the April showers. Their short friendship had been her one great pleasure; but, like the April sunshine, it was soon over; leaving her life, by contrast, darker and more lonely than before. Again she sighed, and whispered softly: "Guy—dear boy—I wish you would come back."

Hark! What is that? Is her wish about to be granted? Is he coming at her call?

A man's rapid step comes towards her through the wood. A turn in the path hides him from view; but the next moment he is in sight, hastening to her.

No; it is not Guy. One glance tells her that. Tall, indeed, he is; but not so tall as Guy; and that dark hair, those flashing black eyes, whose are they? She knows them; but feels well-nigh rooted to the spot with wonder and surprise. Not until he is close upon her—not until he stops before her, holding out both his hands — does Lady Elaine spring up.

"Monty!" she exclaims. "Monty! Can it be?" Then, recovering herself, and slightly drawing back: "Lord Montague, is it really you?"

"So you know me!" he cries, with a joyous laugh, grasping her hands in his, and searching her face eagerly with his keen, dark eyes. "So you know me, Elaine; even after nine long years?"

"Of course I know you, Montague; but you startled me. How did you come? And—and what are you doing here?"

"Well, I came in a train, to begin with," he answers, tightening his hold on her hands as he feels her trying to withdraw them; "then in your dog-cart, which met me at the station; and, as to what I am doing here— just now I am standing talking to you! Why, Elaine, surely you knew I was coming?"

"Knew you were coming! How could I? How should I have known?"

"Surely he told you?"

"Who?"

"Why, your husband. Did he not tell you how we met by chance three days ago, in London; how, strange to say, we made the best of friends, notwithstanding old antipathies; and how he completely buried the hatchet, by asking me down here, to stay as long as I liked? He must have told you."

"He did not tell me," says Lady Elaine quietly. She withdraws her hands from his; turns from him and stoops to pick up her parasol. Since he first came in sight of her, his dark, eager eyes have never left her face, but dwell upon it with the hungry gaze of one who sees at last that which for years he has yearned to look upon. Now she turns away for a moment, and when she looks up again, he is startled to see how deathly pale she has become.

"Elaine," he says, coming quite close to her, and looking down into her face. "I do not attempt to dissemble with you. I like that man no better, I hate him no less, to-day than I did upon your wedding-day, when *he* stood where *I* should have been, and carried off the prize which *I* had already *won*—which *he* had only *bought*. Don't look frightened, dear; I'll say no more of that. But I could not refuse his proffered friendship, when it gave me a chance of seeing you again, at last. Are you not glad to see me?"

"Of course I am glad to see you, Montague," she answers mechanically, stooping as she speaks to pick up some flowers which had dropped from her lap when she rose so hurriedly. "But you startled me, and I am so surprised. Let us go back to The Towers. How did you know I was here?"

"Your carriage returned soon after I arrived," he says, as they walk on together; "the man told me you were coming home through the woods. How fortunate I did not miss you!"

She makes no reply, and he quietly talks for both. When they reach the old beech-tree he stops.

"What a charming view!" he says; "and this mossy bank would make a good seat. You look tired, Elaine. Shall we sit down here and rest a bit?"

"No, not here," she answers hurriedly. "I really want to go home. It looks like rain. Let us make haste."

He says no more until they reach the stile; then gives her his hand to help her over. But on the other side he pauses, still holding her hand tightly in his.

"Ellie," he says, speaking low and tenderly, "do you remember our last parting? Surely you have not forgotten it. Have you nothing warmer for me, now we meet again, than a mere handshake, and this cold, formal greeting? I expected more than that, for the sake of 'auld lang syne.'"

He bends his head so near her as he speaks, that his black moustache almost touches her cheek.

She starts back, and draws her hand from

his; a crimson flush rising to her face, a moment before so pale.

"Lord Montague," she says, her voice quivering with indignation, "you forget yourself! You forget both my position and your own. You are my husband's friend and guest. *I* am his *wife*. Kindly bear that in mind for the future."

She trembles violently, and leans against the stile for support; but he can see she means what she says.

Lord Montague bites his lip, and forces a smile; but the smile is a bitter one.

"Really, I beg your pardon, Lady Elaine. But you misunderstand me. I only remembered that we are—or used to be—cousins. I suppose I erred in thus claiming relationship, after nine years' absence. You must forgive the indiscretion."

She answers not, but passes down the path, he walking just behind; her cousin— her *lover* of former years.

How dark everything looks; how cheerless and gloomy. The sun has vanished behind the clouds, and rain is near. And Lady Elaine knows, within her heart, that in the very place where before she had found the Sunshine, she has now met her life's dark Shadow.

But she walks on calmly; and he follows behind her.

CHAPTER XVII.

"WHAT a strange coincidence, Muriel, that you should have met them!"

Lady Elaine reclined in a garden chair under the cedar. Muriel Bruce sat on a low seat at her feet; and, as they talked, rested her head against her friend's knee; the old favourite attitude so well remembered by Cyril Branscome. She had just been telling Elaine of the evening in the Swiss hotel, when Guy and Cyril came in late, and sat down opposite her at *table d'hôte*.

"And what did you think of Sir Guy?" inquired Lady Elaine presently.

"Oh, I liked the look of him immensely. He is very much what I had imagined, only not quite so boyish as I should have expected, from your account of the amusing way you first made his acquaintance in the wood. I thought him a handsome manly-looking young fellow; but what struck me most was the peculiar sweetness of his smile, and the frank look in his eyes. One felt directly that one could trust him so easily. I quite made up my mind to try and make friends with him the next day, on the ground of our both knowing you, and then to tell him that I knew—that I had once known—Cyril. But, as I told you, they left Vevey quite early the next morning. We never came across them again."

"You seem to have quite lost your heart to Sir Guy," said Lady Elaine, with a half laugh. "It really is a pity you were not shut up together in some dull little Swiss place in wet weather. Something might have come of it. I believe he is very susceptible!"

"Hush!" whispered Muriel, a shade passing over her sweet face. "You know I have no heart to lose; it remains where it was first given, although no longer prized or wanted there. But I know I should like Sir Guy, if I knew him. By the way, Elaine, how came he to set off abroad so suddenly, and stay away so long? It seems rather strange, just after coming into this property, too."

"Oh, it was not so very sudden! His mother had talked of it for some time; though certainly he made up his own mind rather hastily, and lost no time in starting."

"You must rather have missed him," continued Muriel. "From your letters to me, you appeared to be seeing so much of him just then, and you have not many people about here worth knowing."

"Yes, I did miss him," said Lady Elaine.

The two friends sat silent for awhile, each deep in her own thoughts, yet enjoying one another's silent sympathy. It has been said: "The truest test of friendship is to be able to sit or walk together for a whole hour in perfect silence, without wearying of one another's company."

Muriel, as was her wont, sat very still, her hands clasped round her knees, her whole attitude bespeaking a calm peaceful mind; a shadow of sadness was on her face, and the far-away look in her sweet eyes showed her thoughts to be back in a distant past.

Elaine, whose fingers were always restless, with one hand stroked the brown hair at her knee, while the other toyed with a mass of hothouse flowers lying on the rustic table beside her. At last she broke the silence.

"Muriel dearest," she said gently, bending over her friend; "are you quite sure Cyril Branscome really had your letter?"

"Quite sure, Ellie. I gave it to Martha to give him as soon as he arrived, when she let him in. She waited about in the hall for some time, lest one of the other servants should answer the bell when he rang; and she told me afterwards, when I questioned her, that she gave it him at once. I hoped he would be long enough alone in the study to be able to read it before papa came in; but if not, he must have read it directly he left the house."

"But really, Muriel, his conduct has always seemed to me so strange and unaccountable. I cannot help thinking there must have been some sort of misunderstanding. Are you sure you clearly explained exactly how you were circumstanced?"

"Quite clearly. I remember every word of my letter. I told him all about papa's peculiar mental state; how the doctor warned us that the least excitement would most probably either utterly derange his mind or bring on another attack which must be fatal; how he had said, that very morning, that papa was to be crossed in nothing, if we could possibly help it. Then I explained to him how angry papa was about his letter; because he had set his heart on my marrying Mr. Searl, and had never supposed Cyril and I cared for each other. I told him how he raved about it, and accused poor mamma of having encouraged Cyril without his knowledge, and declared he would never hear of my accepting him; and how at last, for my mother's sake, I promised to humour him about it, for the time. Elaine, how could I let my hopes, or my happiness, or my wish to be engaged to Cyril, cost my father his reason, perhaps his life? Besides, I knew it could not be a very long waiting time. They scarcely thought then he would live six months. I told him this, and then—then I told him how much I still loved him, and how I should always be his and his only; and how, though my duty to my parents obliged me to give up for awhile the joy of being openly engaged to him, yet I should think of him every day, and long for the time when nothing should stand between us." Muriel turned and hid her face in her friend's lap. "Oh, Ellie," she murmured, "it is dreadful to think how freely I wrote, and how I let him see my heart! But I thought I could trust him; I thought he loved me, and would wait."

"My dear child," said Lady Elaine decidedly, "he cannot have received your letter. Now, just give me leave to write and ask him whether he ever had it."

Muriel shook her head. "No, no, indeed you must not. Why, supposing it never reached him, surely he would have written to ask me whether I really meant the refusal I had to give him in the study. He would not have given me up so easily as all that. In my letter I arranged a way by which we could write to one another, he enclosing his letters to my mother. I begged him to write at once, that I might know he understood, and did not think I had done wrong, or mind too much having to wait. But day after day went by, and there never came word or sign from him; and at last I heard from mutual friends that he had given up his curacy, and they believed he was travelling abroad. He cannot have loved me much, Elaine"—Muriel's lips quivered and her eyes filled with tears—"he cannot have loved me much, to be angry and give me up at the first difficulty that came in the way. I never saw him again till that night at Vevey. My mother often wanted to find out his address and write to him about it, but I would not let her. I am not very proud, Elaine"—with a mournful little smile—"but what pride I have always rises at the recollection of all I wrote in that letter. Then last year we heard he was at home again, and seeking a tutorship; and, as you know, I wrote to you about it."

"Well," said Lady Elaine, after a pause, "it is a sad story, poor darling; but comfort yourself with the thought that it is not so miserable as mine. At least, you suffer no degradation — no daily, hourly yoke of bondage. All this might have been your lot had you married, as his love for you does not appear to have been worthy of the name. Let us hope you will some day meet one who will make you happy, and care for you, dear, as you deserve."

Muriel shook her head.

"How crooked things do go in this sad, sad world!" sighed Lady Elaine presently, taking up a lovely white azalea from the table as she spoke. "Those whose lot is cast together care nothing for each other, and, as a rule, would be much better far apart; and those who really love us, and would soothe our hearts and make us happy, can be nothing to us. It's a cruel, crooked world, Muriel!"

She fastened the azalea in her dress, then rose wearily from her seat.

Muriel rose also, and, after a moment's hesitation, said gently:

"I wonder you let him stay here so often, Elaine. Considering all there once was between you, it hardly seems right."

"Stay here! Who?"

"Why, Lord Montague."

"Montague! My dear child, I was not thinking of *him!*"

"Of whom, then?" asked Muriel; but Lady Elaine was half-way across the lawn, and did not heed the question.

Muriel picked up her hat and slowly followed her into the house.

CHAPTER XVIII.

How pleasant it is, on a hot Sunday morning, after a dusty walk in the glaring heat of a bright July sun, to find one's self at last in a cool, dimly-lighted church!

So it seemed to Lady Elaine, on the Sunday following her talk with Muriel, as she entered the little church and passed to her usual seat in the chancel. It felt delightfully cool—even the slightly damp smell was refreshing to-day; and the "dim religious light," entering so softly through the stained glass windows, rested and soothed the eyes after the white glare of the dusty roads. The great oak door at the bottom of the church stood open making a dark frame for the green waving trees in the churchyard beyond; and through it a subdued hum—bringing to the mind a general idea of bees, flowers, and sunshine—came stealing in, mingled with the tinkle of sheep-bells, the distant laughter of children, and the voices of the old farmers who assembled in the churchyard before service, congratulating one another on this glorious hay weather.

All this had a very soothing effect upon Lady Elaine on this peaceful Sunday morning, and she felt glad she had come, although Muriel, pleading a bad headache, had left her to do so alone. She leaned back in her corner with closed eyes, and a sense of calm and rest stole over her.

Somehow to-day it all reminded her very much of the little church at her old home, and of how she used to feel on summer Sundays then. There was exactly this same curious damp smell, peculiar to consecrated buildings, which always makes one think of mould and straw hassocks; and there also the Earl's family pew was in the chancel. In fancy she could see herself, a gold-haired little maiden, by her mother's side, standing on the great red hassocks, and leaning forward to peep surreptitiously at little boy-friends from behind the big pillar. Ah! and Montague was one of them! How dark his head used to look even then, beside those of all the stupid little fair boys; and how his black eyes would sparkle back at her, whenever she managed to peep round and send him a smile.

Memory followed upon memory; and, dreaming thus, she did not notice that the organ had begun to wheeze—had given that spasmodic gasp with which it always commenced work for the day, that the droning voluntary was slowly labouring on its weary way. Neither did she hear the rustle of Mrs. Mervyn's silk dress, as she passed up the chancel; nor the strong, firm tread that followed her ; nor the slight stir among the congregation as Bones and the Vicar left the vestry and processioned to the desk.

'*When the wicked man* ——'

Lady Elaine started as Mr. Drawler's loud sonorous voice broke suddenly in upon her reverie. She rose slowly, and opened her Prayer-Book, making a mental effort to recall her thoughts to the present time and place. Whether or not she would have succeeded in doing so remains a doubtful question, had she not happened just then to glance across the chancel. Perhaps Beryl's beaming face attracted her attention ; perhaps a pair of blue eyes, which had been earnestly regarding her for the last five minutes, at length magnetised her into looking up ; anyway, she looked—and saw Guy Mervyn on the opposite side, standing between his mother and Berry.

* * * * *

" Is the head better, Muriel ?"

"How you startled me, Elaine!" cried Muriel, sitting up on the sofa and pushing back her tumbled hair. "You came in so softly, and I had no idea you had returned from church. Yes. thank you, it is much better. I think I have been asleep—dreaming. But are you not in very early?"

"A little sooner than usual, perhaps. The service was rather short, and I walked home quickly across the fields. It is not nearly so hot now as when I started; there is a lovely breeze. It will do you good; let me open your window."

Lady Elaine drew back the curtains, and threw the window wide open; then came and sat on the couch by Muriel's side.

"My dear child," she said anxiously, "how poorly you look; so pale, and with such heavy eyelids. Is anything the matter, besides the headache?"

"No. no," answered Muriel quickly, trying to smile, though the tears would start unbidden; "I shall soon be all right again, Elaine. I am very — foolish. I think it must have been our long talk the other day; but somehow I cannot keep from thinking of a certain person, and of — what might have been. I felt just like this the day before we met him in Switzerland. I am sure he must be near me now"—Lady Elaine turned away her head, to hide a smile—" or ill," went on Muriel, "or dying, or *dead* perhaps." At this dismal climax, her tears overflowed. "Elaine, I think he must be dead, and his spirit is influencing mine."

"Nonsense, my dear Muriel! Do you know that is a particularly unfortunate remark to make to me to-day, as I will soon explain. You must not be so morbidly superstitious, or I shall not tell you something you will be very much interested to hear. Do you know, you missed a great deal by not coming to church with me this morning."

Muriel looked incredulous. "I can't believe that, Elaine; unless, for once, someone else preached instead of Mr. Drawler."

"Well, for once someone else did preach; a young clergyman who has never preached in our church before."

"Was it a good sermon?"

"Very good, I should think. I cannot say I listened much. Mr. Drawler has got one into such a confirmed habit of never attempting to do so. Besides, I was thinking more of the man himself than of what he was saying."

Muriel began to look interested.

"Really! Why? Was he at all remarkable?"

"No, not exactly."

"What was he like? You make me quite curious, Elaine. It is so unusual for you to take interest in anyone."

"He was decidedly good-looking; tall

and fair, with a high white, thoughtful forehead, and a slight stoop. He wore glasses, and had a fine musical voice."

Suddenly the colour rushed in one crimson flood over Muriel's face. "What was his name?" she said.

"The Rev. Cyril Branscome. Now, don't be upset, darling. I knew you must hear of it sooner or later, and thought it best to tell you at once, myself. He has come back from abroad with Guy. They were both in church, and Mr. Branscome preached. Muriel dearest, how white you have grown! Lie back on the pillow directly. Yes, have a good cry, poor darling, if you must; it will do you good."

Very tenderly Elaine soothed and comforted her, till she grew calm again. She had never known what it was to love as Muriel loved Cyril; but she had suffered.

"But what shall I do, Elaine?" said

Muriel presently. "I cannot stay here, where I may meet him any day. I must go home to-morrow; I really must."

Lady Elaine considered for a few moments, then said gently: "Muriel dear, why should you go? Why should you not stay and meet Mr. Branscome? You have nothing to be in the least ashamed of; nothing to reproach yourself with. It is he who might well fly from your sweet presence, dearest. And your meeting him here will be so purely accidental; or, at all events, so it will appear to him. Of course he does not know you are here; he does not even know we are friends, or that it was from me the Mervyns heard of him. I cannot help thinking there may be some explanation of his conduct forthcoming. Why run away from the one chance of receiving it, seeing that this loving, forgiving, long-suffering little heart of yours cannot be happy without him? How or where it occurred I cannot say, but I have always thought there must have been some misunderstanding between you two; one of those fatal mistakes which sometimes irreparably spoil two lives, all for want of a simple word of explanation, which mock-modesty or false pride withholds. Your story sounds so improbable. If you read it in a novel, you would say at once, 'How utterly unlikely!'"

"Stranger things happen in real life than in fiction!" said Muriel, with a mournful smile.

"Nevertheless, dear, do take my advice. If you chance to meet, greet him as an old acquaintance; then wait and see how things turn out. But don't run away from me in the very middle of your visit."

"I will stay," said Muriel; "but I shall take good care not to meet him."

"And I shall take very good care you *do*

meet him," thought Lady Elaine to herself; but she smiled, and said nothing.

"And did you speak to Sir Guy afterwards?"

"No. I hurried home directly the service was over, with my mind full of you."

"How disappointed he must have been! I wonder he did not run after you."

"Oh dear no!" said Lady Elaine; "I have no reason to suppose he even remembered me. He did not look once in my direction during the whole service; and when it was over, he appeared to be very busy hunting for his mother's parasol as I passed the pew, and when that was found, for some other imaginary parasol; so I did not catch his eye even then."

"But, Elaine, I thought you and he were such great friends when he went away."

"Oh yes, no doubt," said Lady Elaine carelessly; "but a year is a long time, and boys have short memories."

"I can't think why you always insist upon calling him a *boy*. Is he much altered?"

"Not much, except that, if anything, he seems taller than ever; and he has grown a moustache, which certainly makes him look older, and fortunately does not hide his mouth yet. You have no idea what a sunny smile he always had, Muriel. No matter how sad I was feeling, it used to cheer me, even before he spoke a word."

"I should so much like to know him," Muriel said.

"No doubt we shall meet him before long, and Cyril Branscome with him."

"That would be dreadful!" said Muriel, her whole face lighting up at the thought. "We *must* keep out of his way, Elaine." Then the light died out of her face as she added: "But now Sir Guy is at home again, don't you think *he* will go away?"

"Very likely indeed," answered Elaine, leaning out of the window to pick a spray of jasmine and hide another smile. "To-morrow, I dare say."

"That would be a good thing," said Muriel mournfully.

CHAPTER XIX.

WHY, on lovely summer days, will mortals so provokingly choose the most delightful nooks in the whole wood in which to pass their time—the very mossiest places, where grow the sweetest ferns and the most fragrant flowers? Why will they persist in sitting for hours at a time under our favourite beech-tree, keeping so still, that when one brings out one's wife and young family for an evening gambol among the gnarled roots and tall bracken fern, one comes upon them suddenly, all unawares?

So thought the rabbits during the days following the first Sunday after Guy's return, and really they had some cause for complaint.

Their territory was first invaded on Monday by a mortal with a book and a white parasol, who spent the whole afternoon under the beech-tree. That same evening came a tall young man, in a gray tweed suit, who walked rapidly along the path, stopped short in front of the old tree, looking at it as if he were half afraid of it; then went up close to it, leaned against the trunk, and stood so for a long time, his head bent down, wrapt in thought. Presently he caught sight of a little pile of rubbish, stones and twigs, and dry old beech-nuts, absently gathered off the moss that afternoon by the lady who had been reading, and put together in a small heap. He started, as if afraid of that also; then, stooping down, picked up one of the little twigs and put it in his waistcoat pocket; but, on second thoughts, he took it out again, threw it down, and walked quickly away.

Next day, in the afternoon, came two ladies with parasols and books, who sat for some time reading under the tree; but one of them started at every sound, and ran to hide among the bracken if footsteps were heard approaching. So matters went on for several days, until at last the little rabbits lost all patience, and betook themselves for their romps and gambols to a more secluded part of the wood, leaving these erratic mortals in sole possession of the old beech and its vicinity.

On Thursday afternoon, Lady Elaine and Muriel Bruce went over to Rookwood, to call on Mrs. Joram. They found her full of Guy's return, and of how his very first visit had been to her. Apparently his long absence had by no means diminished good Mrs. Joram's partiality for him.

On their way home the shade of the woods looked far more inviting than the white dusty roads. So they alighted—sent on the carriage, and, entering them by a by-path, strolled leisurely along in the direction of the cornfield, through which lay the nearest way to The Towers. They were both somewhat preoccupied with their own thoughts, and spoke but little. When they reached the turn in the path which brought them in sight of the old beech, they stopped involuntarily.

Leaning against the trunk, looking out over the cornfield, stood Guy Mervyn.

Their footsteps had made no sound on the thick, soft moss; he had not heard them approach, and was evidently quite unconscious of their presence.

Lady Elaine hesitated a moment; then, placing her finger on her lips, she drew Muriel a few steps off the path, to where a fallen tree was lying.

"Let us sit down here," she whispered, "and see whether he comes by this way."

Muriel silently assented, so taken up by her own thoughts that it did not strike her as strange that Elaine should apparently desire to avoid meeting Guy Mervyn. He was alone; then, doubtless, Cyril was gone. The "good thing" she had wished for had come to pass. How could she ever have wished it? Why had she tried to avoid him? If only he were here now, how gladly she would meet him; even if the meeting should cause her fresh pain! No pain, however hard to bear, could be worse than the dull ache of the thought that he had been so near—so near her—and she had not even seen him; and now he was gone—gone!

And Lady Elaine, as she peeped through the hazel trees to where Guy was standing, felt that he and she could not meet again on this particular spot. The sudden sight of him there recalled to her so vividly all that happened when they were last together in this very place. It seemed but yesterday that he was kneeling at her feet pouring out wild words of love—of passionate, undying love—for her. It seemed but yesterday that she turned away and left him there, stretched at full length upon the ground, his face hidden on his arm, full of bitter remorse for his own mad act, which had spoilt their friendship, and could never be undone. She remembered how for days his last words, and the look of utter misery with which they were uttered, had haunted her: "*I* shall never forget." Poor boy! although a whole year has gone by, for his sake they must not meet here.

But just then Guy turned, and came straight down the path towards them. For a moment Elaine thought he would pass by without noticing their retreat; but the next instant he caught sight of them, stopped short, and stood as if rooted to the ground.

Lady Elaine rose, and held out her hand.

Then Guy recovered himself, and came forward quickly, with just his old, bright smile.

"Lady Elaine!" he said, taking her

proffered hand, and grasping it warmly in his own. " What an awful time it is since we last met !"

And as they stood so for one brief moment, his eyes said more plainly than words could have spoken : " Have you forgotten ? Am I forgiven ? May we be friends ?"

And Lady Elaine smiled at him in answer, and simply said :

" I am glad you have come back at last, Sir Guy."

And thus they met again.

" I must introduce you to Miss Bruce," said Lady Elaine. " Muriel, you have heard me speak of Sir Guy Mervyn."

Guy turned to her with a smile.

" I believe we have met before ?" he said.

" This time I can answer, *yes*," said Muriel, laughing.

" How cruelly you snubbed me at Vevey, for my mistake," said Guy. " Across the table, too ! I felt terribly small, and devoutly wished the earth would open and swallow me up! And it was a very natural mistake to make, was it not? I never forget a face; and I had seen such a lifelike portrait of you on Lady Elaine's writing-table."

"But, indeed, Sir Guy," protested Muriel, "I did not mean to snub you. I so wished afterwards that I had been more sociable; but I was rather — rather preoccupied that evening. It was so stupid of me, too; for I guessed who you were. Elaine had told me about you, and had mentioned that you were travelling abroad."

They both knew how Muriel had in reality known him; so it did not strike them that this was rather a lame way of accounting for the recognition.

"Fancy!" said Lady Elaine, looking up at him as he stood before them. "Fancy this young man pretending to feel small! What effrontery!"

"Bodily size," remarked Guy, with mock

gravity, "greatly aggravates the agony when one is feeling mentally small."

"How you must suffer, then!" laughed Elaine, looking almost proudly at his splendid figure and broad shoulders. How glad she felt to have him back! just the same bright merry Guy as of old; so utterly unaltered —so perfectly unconstrained and natural in manner—that, were it not for that one questioning look, she would have thought he must have entirely forgotten how they had last parted. There was the old smile, which always warmed her heart like sunshine; and the same straightforward open look in those blue eyes, revealing a nature above deceit, above all mean pettiness, having nothing to be ashamed of, nothing to conceal.

The old feeling rose up strongly in her heart: that which she had always more or less felt for him, since she lectured him and gave him advice, and he cared so much for her opinion; a sort of feeling of his belonging in a way to her, which seemed to give her a right to be proud of him, and used to make her like to say "my dear boy" sometimes, when she spoke to him; although half conscious all the while that he was not exactly a boy, and that she herself was rather young to be so maternal with him. And what wonder that she had grown to care for him, when she had so little to love, and he was so lovable and so loving? But it had been a mistake— a great mistake, and brought sore trouble to poor Guy, and pain to her own heart; and now, as Guy appeared to have returned quite heart-whole and sensible, she must be much more discreet, and allow no sentimentality to grow up between them; and it was very sweet to have him back again; and — who shall say?—perhaps, even to Lady Elaine, the remembrance of that romantic episode beneath the old beech added an unconscious charm to their friendship, and deep down in her heart rose the unspoken, unacknowledged thought: " Does he, I wonder, love me still?"

" Perhaps you will share our seat for a little while, Sir Guy, unless you have to hasten home?"

"I am in no hurry, Lady Elaine;" and Guy seated himself on one end of the fallen trunk as he spoke. "In fact, I have been waiting here some time for my friend Cyril Branscome, whom I am expecting every moment."

Muriel rose hastily, then sat down again.

" He is afflicted with a mania for botany," continued Guy, "which I do not share; and has gone off to the marsh after some rare and peculiar species of duckweed, which he hears is to be found there. I had something to do in another direction, but our ways converged just here; so we made the old beech a rendezvous, and agreed to meet at five o'clock. Cyril calls himself the soul of punctuality, and it is now quite twenty minutes past; so, duckweed or no duckweed, he must soon be here."

"I am glad of that," said Lady Elaine, "for I want to meet Mr. Branscome. We will wait till he arrives, in order to make his acquaintance, and hear all about the duckweed."

Muriel rose again, took up her parasol, and said hurriedly:

"Don't mind me, Elaine, or think of coming back on my account; but I really must go home now. I had no idea it was so late. You know, I have those letters to write before post-time."

"I know nothing of the kind!" said Lady Elaine decidedly, ignoring Muriel's piteous look of entreaty. "This is the first I have heard of 'those letters'! I cannot let you be so unsociable, just when we have got Sir Guy here to amuse us. Besides, you are so fond of botany, and ought to be interested in rare duckweed. Really, Muriel, you shall not go off and write imaginary letters on such a lovely afternoon."

"But indeed I must, Elaine. One is to my mother. I shall lose the post. Good-bye. No, I can't wait!" And she hurried away.

"Let me just help you over the stile, Miss Bruce!" shouted Guy; and before she reached it, he overtook her.

As he gave her his hand he said gently:

"I do wish you could stay a little while. I should like you to meet my friend Cyril Branscome. He is one in a thousand—a really splendid fellow!"

The colour rushed into her face, and he thought there were tears in the sweet eyes raised to his. She opened her lips and tried to speak, but the words would not come. Without any answer she turned from him, and ran lightly across the field. And Guy climbed the bank and went slowly back, his heart full of generous gladness. "She loves him," he said to himself; " dear old fellow, he may be happy yet!"

Lady Elaine was really vexed with Muriel; not only for thus running away from her own chances of happiness, but for leaving her to a *tête-à-tête* in the wood with Guy. She had felt Muriel's presence to be a good thing for them both at this first meeting; and now, as she saw Guy returning alone, she feared lest recollections, which surely must occur to him as he passed the beech-tree, should make him shy and constrained with her, and set up a barrier between them which might prevent their friendship in the future.

But no such thoughts seemed to be troubling Guy as he sat down beside her, saying:

" I wish she could have stayed."

" Yes," said Lady Elaine; then added, after a moment's thought: " I may as well tell you, the fact is, she and Cyril Branscome are old acquaintances."

"I knew that already."

"Ah!" Lady Elaine glanced at him quickly, trying to discover what more he knew. "And is Mr. Branscome aware that she is a friend of mine, and likely to be staying here?"

"He has no idea of it," Guy replied. "You remember asking me not to mention our having heard of him through you, or that you knew anything about him? So, when I accidentally discovered that his "—Guy hesitated—" his friend was your friend also, I understood that, to carry out your wish, I must not tell him so, without your permission; though, I confess, I have many times been tempted to do so."

"That was very good indeed of you, and very discerning, too. Perhaps you also guessed who asked me to recommend him to you, and who was so anxious for news of him when he arrived?"

"I did," said Guy; "and that is what I so much wished to tell him."

"Would he have cared to know?"

"I think he would. May I tell him now?"

"No, please don't just yet. I do want them to meet, and renew their old acquaintance. Let us give him a surprise. Cannot you bring him to The Towers to-morrow afternoon? Come about four, and stay to tea; then we can all become mutually acquainted. I should much like to hear where you have been all this time, and what you have been doing. Now, no excuses! Do come!"

"Thank you," said Guy, "we certainly will."

"And what has Mr. Branscome told you about Muriel Bruce?" asked Lady Elaine presently.

Guy smiled, and shook his head.

"No, no, Lady Elaine, that won't do! I

must be true all round. If I keep your secrets, I must keep Cyril's also; and you must be generous, and not pump me; for it is so awfully hard to refuse you anything. Perhaps, soon, there will be no need for any secrets."

"I trust so," she answered; and both were silent, she thinking of her friend—he, of his.

"How crooked most things go, in this world!" remarked Elaine at length with a sigh; "don't you think so?"

"I thought so a year ago," Guy answered in a low voice; not looking at her as he spoke, and busily punching little holes with his stick in the turf at his feet. "Yes, I certainly thought so a year ago. But since then I have found out something which makes all crooked things go straight."

He looked up at her now, and the joy shining in his eyes, the bright look of true gladness on his face, made her say quickly:

"Why, Guy! What is it? I thought something had come to you. In most ways you seem quite unaltered; but once or twice while we have been talking here, and in church on Sunday, I have noticed a sudden look of gladness come into your face, as though you had just remembered something so delightful that all else, whether pleasant or annoying, is as nothing compared with it. Now tell me what it is! Tell me, Guy!"

She spoke earnestly, and leaned towards him, awaiting his answer; her hand lightly resting on his arm.

Why does he not speak? Why can he not tell her, now the time has come, what he has longed for months to let her know? How often he has said to himself: "If only she knew!" But now that she has asked him—now that she sits waiting to hear it from his lips—it seems too much for him; he knows if he tries to speak his voice will tremble; and when a man feels that, he invariably takes refuge in silence.

"I know!" cried Elaine suddenly. "I guess! You are in love!"

She said it with conviction, and yet half incredulous.

"Yes," said Guy, speaking slowly and quietly. "I have given my heart to some-one."

"Really? And is your love returned?"

"Not exactly returned," he answered, smiling, "for I love because I was loved first."

"What a remarkable state of things! However, you seem very happy over it. And may I know who—but look, is not this Mr. Branscome?"

"Yes," said Guy. "Here we are, Cyril!"

Then in a low tone, for Cyril was close upon them, he added hurriedly: "It is not at all what you think; but I will tell you all to-morrow."

"You mysterious young man!" she said; and he answered with his own bright smile, as they rose together and went to meet Cyril Branscome.

CHAPTER XX.

"Preposterous!"

Gertrude's indignant tones, entering at the open window, reached Guy and Cyril as they sat at work in Guy's little sanctum.

Cyril was seated at the table, his head in his hands, poring over an interesting old volume he had found in the library. Guy lounged on his favourite couch, in an attitude betokening the heat of the day and the dulness of his book. He had amused himself for the last five minutes with shooting little paper pellets at his more studious friend; but they entirely failed to arouse Cyril, no matter where they struck, and lay unnoticed on the table around him. So Guy tried a fresh attitude, in which his heels were considerably higher than his head; and finding this position decidedly inspiring, turned his attention to his book once more.

"Preposterous!"

This time Gertrude's voice sounded louder and still more indignant. She was crossing the lawn just opposite the window, and retreating with dignity into the house.

At the exclamation, both young men looked up, exchanging an amused smile, as Berry's wicked little laugh sounded in the distance. The next moment Berry herself danced by the window, only pausing an instant as she passed to peep in, and jerk her thumb over her right shoulder, after the manner of old Frost, the gardener, whispering with a grimace: "*Pre*-pos-terous!"

"Hullo, Berry!" shouted Guy, sitting up; "come here."

"Well?" said Berry demurely, reappearing, and standing on the gravel walk outside.

"What is preposterous?" inquired Guy.

"My blessed boy, don't you know! That is Gertrude's last new word, at sound of which we are all to feel crushed and annihilated. She always has one going, especially for my benefit."

Guy laughed.

"You graceless little sinner! You look neither crushed nor annihilated. Does she, Cyril? But what's the row? What have you been saying or doing, to call forth the awful word?"

"I can't tell you from out here," whispered Beryl. "Mother is in the boudoir, with the window open. She hears of my misdeeds quite soon enough from Gerty, without my publishing them, myself, to the world at large."

"Come up the bank then, and put your head in at the window."

"So I would, Guy; but you insist on that climbing rose being allowed to grow rampant all over the place. It's chock-full of earwigs, and I can't abide them!"

"Nonsense, Berry; earwigs won't eat you! Come up directly, or I shall call you a little——"

"No, no! I am coming, Guy," cried Beryl, anxious to maintain her reputation for courage; and soon her merry face appeared at the window, all among the yellow roses.

"You big lazy boy! Fancy sprawling on the sofa, with your coat off, in that fashion! I'm ashamed of you."

"My dear child, I am studying," said Guy, with dignity; "and proving how true it is that 'much study is a weariness to the flesh.' But don't stand there lecturing other people, Miss Berry. Confess your own evil deeds instead. How came you thus to offend our elder sister?"

"Why, I only said I had told little Percy Flamingo that if he wished to stand any chance of winning Gerty's heart he must wear a white tie. You know, Gerty dotes on white ties. Remember the curate at Granton. Why, a cabinet photograph of him stood on her dressing-table for months, till I painted him a red choker, and gave him a blear look in the eye. I couldn't help it, Guy; he did look so foolishly sanctimonious, with his long black coat almost down to his heels, like a be-draggled blackbird; and holding on to a greasy smile, which evidently went slipping—slipping, while you could almost hear the photographer count—one—two—three; and he had one foot out, and an open Bible in his hand—which, by the way, wasn't a Bible at all, you know, but a dirty old copy of Robinson Crusoe; everyone is done with the same, at that shop at Granton. Well, he was presenting Robinson Crusoe to you with one hand, and laying the other on his heart. I got quite sick of seeing him when I slept in Gerty's room. But, oh! he looked fine with the choker and that expression in the eye! My dear boy, I made another man of him! (Only Gerty did not seem to think so, and shed many tears over him, and put him away in a drawer.) Then there was Cyril. Oh yes, Cyril; she was awfully sweet on you, till Guy took you off out of harm's way; but you need not feel in the least flattered or gratified; it was solely on account of your white tie."

Cyril leaned back in his chair and laughed heartily.

"I declare," went on Berry, "were he not married already, I really believe she would fall in love with the old wicked man himself."

"With *whom*, Berry?"

"Why, don't you know? That is my name for Mr. Drawler. I call him so because he begins every service always, without exception, with 'When the wicked man,' and he brings it out with such gusto, as though calling us all *wicked men* gave him real satisfaction. But I was telling you about Percy Flamingo. He has appeared lately in a tie which Gerty thinks is a white one. It isn't really; it is meant to have lots of little yellow spots on a white ground, but they have faded in the wash. However, this morning, while we were gardening, Gerty sentimentally remarked that *dear* little Percy wore a white tie now. I said of course he did, as I had told him it was the only way to win her. She called that *preposterous*, and went indoors, furiously declaring that she will compel me this afternoon, when they come, to confess that it was a 'pure fabrication' of my own, and a 'preposterously silly joke,' or she will tell him so herself!"

"You bad child," said Guy, laughing; then he added, more seriously: "But really, Berry dear, you do tease poor Gerty shamefully. I think it is a little too bad sometimes."

"Not a bit!" cried Berry indignantly; "she deserves it. Only think how she plagues me, and how she used to go on at you, till you went and grew that little moustache, and looked altogether grown up. But, Guy "—a little quiver came into Berry's voice—" I sometimes feel now as though you are quite giving me up. You always take Gerty's part, though you used to tease her as much as anyone in old days; and last night, after I went up to bed, I saw you walking up and down the lawn in the moonlight talking for nearly an hour, and you had your arm round her shoulders. I cried myself to sleep with jealousy."

"Nonsense, little one!" said Guy, getting up and going to the window; "you ought to know better than to be jealous of anyone. But I think we must give up having fun at Gerty's expense, which causes her real pain and mortification. Chaff Cyril and me as much as you like; we can pay you back in your own coin. But poor old Gerty will never learn to understand a joke, and take it as it is meant. And, by the way, did you really say that to Percy Flamingo about the white tie?"

"Of course not, Guy. So you may think how delicious it will be to hear Gerty explaining, and denying, and incriminating me; while poor little Percy stands bewildered before her, screwing his eye-glass first into one eye, then into the other, and vaguely twisting and twirling his imaginary moustache; and then, to crown all, he will have to confess that it would have been *yellow*, only the spots washed out!"

Berry went off into an uncontrollable peal of laughter at the thought; then suddenly cried: "Guy, look!—an earwig!—on that rose close to your head!" and fled down the path; while Guy laughingly picked the rose and flung it after her.

"What a child!" he said, turning to Cyril. "She grows no older! Twelve months, and the extra inches to her petticoats, of which she is so proud, haven't made a bit of difference; she is as full of fun and mischief as ever."

"She's a little brick!" said Cyril warmly. "Why should you wish her any different? And beneath all that frolicsome flow of irrepressible spirits, she has the warmest, truest heart that ever beat. I can see she loves you, old fellow, with that sort of love which, if needs be, lays down life with a smile. And she has a wonderfully quick perception, and clear, unerring penetration; and knows how to use them, too, when those she loves are concerned."

"Dear little woman!" Guy said tenderly.

"Joking apart," Cyril went on, "I really believe if I had come here heart-whole, I might have privately fallen in love with your little Berry, and silently waited till short petticoats grew into long ones."

"My dear fellow!" Guy looked positively aghast. "Surely such an idea never entered your head, as that our little madcap Berry could ever grow into a *clergyman's* wife, if she lived to be a hundred! Why, like the old woman of historic renown, if she 'lived to a hundred and ten, she'd die of a fall from a cherry-tree then.' Berry a parson's wife— a vicar's wife—like Mrs. Drawler, say, with mothers' meetings, and soup-tickets, and choirs, and anthems, and gruel for old women, all under her care! My dear old chap, it takes one's breath away!"

"Well," Cyril said, half in play, half in earnest, "and why not? A clergyman's wife needs a fund of good spirits, though Paul does say 'the deacons' wives must be grave'; and I should think, in dealing with a lot of crotchety old people, a sense of the humorous would not come amiss. But, my dear boy, I have no designs on Berry; so don't look so horrified. As you know, I never intend to marry, or pin my happiness on any woman again."

"Well," said Guy, "let me tell you Berry's last prank, and then think of her as an embryo clergyman's wife, if you can! Having an idle hour yesterday morning, she ransacks an old wardrobe filled with things my mother has not yet had time to look over; and, as luck will have it, finds a pair of black trousers of my uncle's. Apparently old Sir Guy was unusually large and rotund. Berry promptly arrays herself in these garments, with a pillow behind and a pillow in front, 'for stuffing,' you know; then puts a white cloth over her head, and makes her way, unnoticed, to the top of a sort of cupboard staircase leading down into the kitchen. This Berry carefully descends, hind part before, and when she is near the bottom, and well in view—if the door is opened—stands still, and makes an unearthly groaning sound. Old Mrs. Grumball, the housekeeper, happens to be in the kitchen, and opening the door to see what is the matter, comes face to face with

Berry's hind quarters. I believe she promptly went into a fit. The cook fled into the garden, where mother and I happened to be. We went in at once to see what was the matter, and I must say it looked most uncanny. As soon as Berry heard me there, she fled up the stairs with wonderful rapidity for so corpulent an old gentleman. I dashed up after her, and we had a fine chase along the corridors. You never saw anything so funny as Berry running in those pillows, hitching up the trousers as she went! I caught her at last, and brought her back, just as she was, to the kitchen, where mother and the maids were busy bringing Mrs. Grumball round. Poor Berry nearly cried at having to be paraded before them all, for the whole household had assembled — even old Frost came in from the garden. But I thought she really deserved it; besides, nothing else would have convinced them the place was not haunted. As it is, old Mrs. Grumball will not listen to reason, and has given notice to leave as soon as possible. She's a pigheaded old body—like most of her profession; no matter what we said, she always fell back upon: 'Well, it may have bin Miss Berry *this* time, but it will be *the old master next*, and it's not likely *I'm* a-going to wait for *that!*' So the old lady is going, bag and baggage; and though mother looks grieved over it for Berry's benefit, between ourselves, I think she is rather pleased; for she found Mrs. Grumball a tartar to manage, and hardly liked to sack her after so many years of service in this house. So, my dear fellow, next time Berry occurs to you as eminently suited to be a clergyman's wife in the future, picture her to yourself with my uncle's nether garments on, and those pillows! But be sure you never let her know I told you about it. Berry is very particular about some things; and, considering the nature of her attire, she would never forgive me. She remarked afterwards: 'I *am* thankful Cyril was out of the way.' Never hint that you know."

"On my honour, I won't," said Cyril; "but I would give a great deal to have been behind Mrs. Grumball when she opened the staircase door. It must have been a sight never to be forgotten!"

"Well," said Guy, picking up his coat, "I shall have to stop this explanation of Gerty's to young Flamingo, though I make Berry indignant by doing so. He is an arrant little cad, and we can't have his mild attempts at flirtation with Gertrude encouraged. I almost wish we had not settled to go up to The Towers this afternoon, as they are coming for tennis."

"I don't think I shall go," said Cyril. "Your friend only asked me because I turned up, and she could not well avoid doing so. Two is company, three is none; so let me stay and keep an eye on the amorous Flamingo."

"No, no." said Guy quickly; "you must come. Lady Elaine made quite a point of it to me before you arrived. Beside, we should be three anyhow, as she has a friend staying with her."

"Oh! I see," said Cyril. "Then, while you talk to her ladyship, I am to make myself agreeable to the friend? Well, I hope she will not prove very uninteresting, or very lacking in conversational powers. Those sort of young ladies always make me nervous, and I feel inclined to begin reciting Homer or Virgil to them."

"Perhaps she may prove very charming," remarked Guy, looking out of the window.

"Tant mieux!" said Cyril carelessly. "I will go with you. What time?"

"Four o'clock."

"I will be ready."

"He little dreams!" thought Guy.

CHAPTER XXI.

It was no small anxiety to Guy how this meeting between Cyril and his former love would come off.

That same afternoon, as the two young men walked over to The Towers, Guy was revolving the matter in his mind; and, the more he thought of it, the more uneasy he felt. Guy had regretted his promise to Lady Elaine, to give no hint to Cyril of Muriel Bruce's presence at The Towers, ever since he made it. Supposing Cyril found out, as he was almost certain to do, that Guy had known all along who was the friend they were going to meet, would he not be justly indignant with him for having given him no word of warning? Was it quite generous to his friend, quite acting up to the laws of true friendship, to allow him to be ushered—all unprepared—into the presence of this girl, whose changeable fickleness had worked such havoc in his life? On the other hand, Guy had always believed from the first that some explanation must be forthcoming from somewhere, if these two could but meet once more; and nothing, he well knew, would induce Cyril to go to The Towers if he knew Muriel Bruce was there. One thought brought comfort to Guy's perturbed mind. Lady Elaine had made him promise; and Lady Elaine had contrived the meeting. "Women are more far-sighted than men in these matters," he thought to himself; "and, no doubt she will settle it all, in some artful way which has never occurred to me."

"How silent you are, old fellow!"

"Am I?" said Guy, starting, and rousing himself with an effort.

Cyril remembered Guy's sudden confidences to him on the Lake of Geneva, and the name he had accidentally seen in that much-treasured little Bible, and drew his own conclusions.

"This is a fine old park," he said. "What rare good oaks!"

"Yes," answered Guy, "and here we are in sight of the house. What do you think of it?"

"A jolly old place!" said Cyril; "looks as if it might be haunted; dismal in autumn, I should think. So while you talk to her ladyship, Guy, I am to retire and make love to the friend! Is that the programme?"

"Do, by all means," Guy answered dryly.

Lady Elaine was alone in the drawing-room when they were ushered in. She stood at the further end, looking out of the French window, which opened on to the lawn; and, before turning to receive them, she quickly drew down the blind.

As she advanced towards them down the long drawing-room, Guy was forcibly reminded of the night of the dinner-party, so long ago, and of the boyish awe and admiration he then felt at her grace and beauty. She looked more delicate now, and even more transparently white. The soft cream-coloured tea gown she wore hung about her in loose folds, and trailed noiselessly on the carpet behind her. In the silver girdle at her waist were a bunch of yellow roses. A settled sadness was in her eyes and around her lips (Guy had noticed that as they talked together in the woods the day before); but she smiled kindly as she shook hands with them both.

"I am so pleased to see you," she said; "sit down and rest here a little while, until you are cooler; then we will go into the garden. It is really very good of you to have come over on such a hot afternoon."

Just then Guy caught sight of Muriel's

photograph, which usually stood among several others on Lady Elaine's writing-table. It had been placed in a conspicuous position on a table near which they were sitting; so near, indeed, to the chair Cyril had taken, that he had but to turn his head to see it at his elbow.

"You gave us quite a treat on Sunday, Mr. Branscome," said Lady Elaine. "From year's end to year's end we rarely hear any voice but Mr. Drawler's; indeed, I am quite surprised at his asking you to preach, and so soon, too."

"Guy managed that," said Cyril, smiling; "but I fear I shall never be asked again. The Vicar evidently did not like my sermon or agree with the truths I attempted to set forth in it. Did you?" he asked rather abruptly.

Guy looked up eagerly, awaiting her answer.

"Oh, I always agree with all sermons,"

Lady Elaine said carelessly. "It saves so much trouble, and I suppose they are all good in their way, even Mr. Drawler's. And what do you think of our little church? Pretty, isn't it? but shamefully neglected. And the music! You used to be specially critical about that, Sir Guy. Do you think it has improved?"

"It is awful!" cried Guy. "But how can it improve with such a fellow as that schoolmaster for organist? Did you notice in the voluntary on Sunday the pleasing little variety every now and then in the pedal notes, when his toe alighted on B flat instead of C sharp? 'Next best thing, wasn't it, sir?' he said quite cheerfully, when I happened to meet him on Monday, and remarked upon it. Whether this was cheek, or imbecility, I don't quite know; the latter I should think, from his next remark: 'Besides, the best music is full of accidentals, isn't it, Sir Guy?' I didn't know whether to laugh or to kick the fellow."

Lady Elaine smiled.

"It does not do to be too musical in country places. I was so fond of music once, but for years I have not sung a note, or touched my piano. You must let me hear you play your violin, which your little Berry says is 'simply splendid'; perhaps then I may be re-inspired."

As she finished speaking, Lady Elaine glanced meaningly at him, and gave an almost imperceptible nod in Cyril's direction. Guy looked at his friend. Cyril sat as if transfixed, staring at the photograph beside him.

"May I ask whether you know that young lady, Mr. Branscome?"

Even in his anxiety for Cyril, Guy could not help feeling amused at the cool way in which Lady Elaine asked the question. The next moment he was surprised at the unconcerned manner in which Cyril turned and answered; though his colourless face greatly belied the cold indifference of his tone.

"I cannot say I know her; but I *knew* her once—some time ago."

"Indeed! She is a great friend of mine. Do you think that photo is like her?"

Cyril took it up and examined it carefully before he answered.

"I should say it is, so far as I remember; but she was a good deal younger than this, at the time I knew her best. Mr. Bruce was my tutor before I went to Cambridge."

"Really! Just come to the window with me," said Lady Elaine, rising. "Now Mr. Branscome, I will show you the original, and you will be better able to judge."

She touched the cord as she spoke; the blind flew up, and they saw Muriel sitting reading near the cedar-tree. Such a sweet, girlish figure, leaning back in a low garden chair; her hat on her lap, a book in her hand, on which she seemed intent. Her simple black dress became her well; one red rose at her throat was her only ornament. She was evidently utterly unconscious of being observed.

Cyril Branscome looked, but spoke never a word.

Guy, in the background, thought to himself, with admiration: "What heads women have for managing this sort of thing!"

Lady Elaine went on speaking, without looking at Cyril.

"Miss Bruce recognised your name on Sunday, when I told her who was our preacher. So she knows you are in the neighbourhood, and will, I am sure, be pleased to meet you. Let us join her under the cedar. It is pleasantly shady there."

She stepped out of the window. Cyril and Guy walked beside her; and, as they crossed the space which intervened between them and the girl to whom Cyril's whole heart had gone out with a sudden bound, he—manlike—was hardening that heart and bringing it in check again, by repeating to himself her last cruel words to him: "I cannot accept your offer, Mr. Branscome, and I do not wish you to try to see me, or press it further."

Poor Muriel!

She heard them coming and looked up; then started to her feet, the colour rushing into her cheeks at sight of him. But her womanly pride came to the rescue. She was quite calm and composed as she laid down her book and came towards them; she even stopped and put in a marker before closing the book.

"You need not introduce us, Elaine— unless Mr. Branscome has forgotten me. We are quite old friends."

Those sweet, wistful eyes are looking into his; the hand he used to hold for hours in the firelight is once more held out to him.

"You do me too great an honour, Miss

Bruce, by preserving any recollection of me. I was but one among many."

He alone knew the full meaning of his own words; and even he wished them unsaid the moment they were uttered. But Muriel, innocent of having ever cared for another, or of having even thought of any other man as a lover, answered simply:

"It is true poor papa had a great many pupils; but mother and I made friends with very few. Don't you remember?"

Cyril bowed in answer.

Muriel's colour rose again painfully.

Then Elaine introduced Guy, who concluded, as he and Muriel silently shook hands, that she had forgotten, in the awkward confusion of this first meeting, the fact of their having met before. It never occurred to him to suspect that Lady Elaine had foreseen the probable unpleasantness for him, should Cyril find out that he had known beforehand whom they were to meet; and that she had planned this little stratagem in order to avert any such suspicion. Perhaps had honest Guy guessed this, he would hardly have lent himself to the deception.

"Let us come into the shade," said Lady Elaine; "it is still too hot to be pleasant out on the lawn." Then, as they moved on, she murmured very low to Guy: "For goodness' sake, talk!" Guy began promptly, as though she had touched a spring and set him on by clockwork; though when he commenced he hardly knew what his remark was going to be about.

"What a jolly old tree! Why, it must be shady under there all the year round."

"Yes," said Lady Elaine, smiling; "especially in summer."

"I meant at all times of the day," explained Guy, raising a huge drooping bough, as she passed beneath it. "Why, this is glorious; like a great cool cathedral. Doesn't it beat the cedars of Lebanon, Branscome?"

"Oh!" cried Muriel, turning quickly to him before he could reply. "Have you had your wish? Have you really been to Palestine?"

"Yes, Miss Bruce. I travelled there with young Mr. Rodney two years ago." He answered quietly, without raising his eyes from the ground.

Elaine had taken one of the large garden chairs, and Guy was bringing another forward for Muriel; but she did not notice it. She stood beside Cyril, her cheeks flushed, her eyes sparkling with excitement.

"Oh! how you must have enjoyed it! You always used to say it was the one country you longed most to visit. And we used to plan what you would see and do when you went there, and you said you would never get the chance; but I always felt certain you would, some day. Don't you remember how often we talked about it?"

Then Cyril raised his eyes, and looked

full into hers, as he answered coldly: "Oh, did we?"

Muriel looked like a child who has been cruelly struck for no fault, yet can neither resist nor question. Her eyes fell before his, and she turned away. Guy shot an angry look at Cyril; but he had picked up a fir cone, and was examining it minutely. Lady Elaine drummed impatiently on the rustic table beside her with her restless white fingers.

"Muriel darling, come and sit here by me. Sir Guy is going to tell us all sorts of amusing stories about Spain and Italy. He is not, like Mr. Branscome, absorbed in his own thoughts, but has time to attend to us ladies."

"I beg your pardon," said Cyril, throwing away the fir cone and turning towards her as he heard his own name. "Did you speak to me?"

"Oh no!" said Lady Elaine sharply.

"Oh dear no! *I* did not speak. But Miss Bruce was talking to you just now; and you appeared too much preoccupied to hear what she said."

"I heard what Miss Bruce said, Lady Elaine."

"Indeed! Then you have a very short memory, Mr. Branscome."

He did not answer. Poor Muriel coloured painfully, and looked about for some way of escape.

Guy came to the rescue.

"Now, Lady Elaine, I can't have you scold my friend for his absence of mind. That is my own special prerogative; and, though I make his life a burden to him sometimes myself, I don't like to hear him pitched into by anyone else. He is awfully absent-minded, and some day, when he is not by, I will tell you and Miss Bruce a few of the pranks Berry has played on him; they are really worth hearing. Have you seen my little Berry since the girls came home, Lady Elaine?"

"Not alone. But she and I made friends before they joined you abroad. Now tell me all about it; where you went, and what you did."

Guy could talk well; and, like most people who talk well, loved talking. He needed no second invitation, and, once launched, kept them thoroughly amused.

Lady Elaine lay back in her low wicker chair, fanning herself with her large garden hat, and watching him with that pleased indulgent smile with which she always looked at Guy when he spoke. Apparently nothing he said could come amiss to Lady Elaine— at all events, on this afternoon.

She, in her turn, was watched by Cyril; who, seated a little way off, and half behind her, eyed her keenly all the while. She knew what had been between him and Muriel—of that he felt certain; and knowing it, considered *him* in the wrong—that was equally evident. What version of the affair had she heard? Cyril would have given much to know, albeit he was telling himself spitefully that it matters little what these silly women say or think; they like to weave their silken fetters round a man, and bind him to their little finger; and when they have enjoyed their power for awhile, and tired of their toy, why then they cast him off; and should he chance to cross their path again in after-years, just in an idle hour when others are not by, no doubt they like to find out, if they can, what havoc they have worked in all his life, and probe his heart with their soft words and softer glances, as though true love had never been, and a broken heart was but a trumpery thing, and pain a passing dream. But to be caught twice in the same net, a man must be a sorry fool. And then he looked past Elaine, and stole a glance at Muriel.

How like the Muriel of old days! how like the Muriel he had loved and lost; only more beautiful, more sweet, more womanly! That tinge of sadness in her face only enhanced its loveliness. Sadness? "Ah yes! she too has suffered," thought Cyril, as he looked at her more closely. "Has she in her turn been jilted, I wonder? Strange that she is not married, not even engaged." For her left hand rested on the arm of her chair, and he could see she wore no ring. Her head was half averted; apparently her whole attention was given to Guy; and, sure of not being observed, Cyril looked—and looked. He only seemed to become conscious now of the hungry longing for a sight of her which had been gnawing at his heart all these long months and years. And as he looked, all else around him faded from his sight. He took in every detail; every line of her face and figure; every wave of that soft brown hair (he had shyly kissed it once, long ago). He looked at her as a man looks his last upon all that is earthly of his best beloved, ere the coffin lid is closed, and the cold corpse shut out from his sight for evermore. It never struck Cyril Branscome that beneath that fair form there beat a living, loving heart, throbbing just now with love for him, and him alone. Nor did it occur to him, seeing she still was free, to try and win her for himself again. As he had told Guy, he was not the man to ask a woman twice; and run the risk of being befooled again. And yet he loved her still, as much, ay, more than ever; but, though his love was strong, so was his pride; so was his *self-love;* and—alas! for poor Muriel —pride and self-love together outweighed even his love for her.

True it is that an early disappointment in love, an early loss of faith in womanhood, develops the worst points in a man's nature, and stunts the upward growth of his nobler instincts, his higher aspirations. Had Cyril been Guy Mervyn, he would have tried now to see Muriel alone, and tell her that he loved her still, and longed unutterably to have her for his own again. Not being Guy Mervyn, not being half so loving, half so unselfishly devoted, half so generous as Guy would have been in his place, he steeled his heart against her; told himself, again and again, that a man must be a sorry fool to be caught twice by the same woman, and thought bitterly of the day when he had stood before this girl and been refused.

Just then his eye chanced to rest on the red rose she wore at her throat, her only ornament. It was fastened there by a little old silver brooch; a birthday gift of *his* to her, long years ago.

"Did Guy really do it, Mr. Branscome?"

Lady Elaine was quietly watching him from beneath her long lashes.

"Did Guy really do it, Mr. Branscome?"

Poor Cyril was quite at sea; and his inward thoughts about her ladyship were not exactly complimentary.

"Er—yes; he did."

"Oh, really! and what did you think of such a mad proceeding?"

"She is doing this on purpose, I know," thought Cyril. But they were waiting for his answer; even Muriel turned and looked at him. "What did I think of what?" he said, rather incoherently.

"Why, what I was telling them," put in Guy. "It is too much for Lady Elaine's credulity. She appeals to you for confirmation."

"I am afraid I did not hear"—began Cyril apologetically.

"Oh, never mind, Mr. Branscome," interposed Lady Elaine. "You were not listening, were you? No. I thought not.

You were studying Muriel's rose, weren't you? Oh, I know you are fond of botany. Guy told me that yesterday. So when we have had tea, which I see they are just bringing out, I will ask Muriel to take you to the orchid house. She is fond of botany also, and is most enthusiastic over our orchids. She will tell you all their names, which is more than I could do. Do you take sugar?"

By this time poor Muriel's cheeks were scarcely less, red than the unfortunate rose, and Cyril's confusion was nearly as great. Guy was dying to laugh. Elaine's apparent unconsciousness of the effect produced by her words; the perfectly innocent look of inquiry in her sweet grey eyes, as she paused —sugar-tongs in hand—and looked at Cyril, were too much for Guy. He had never seen Lady Elaine 'score off' anyone before, and his sense of humour was tickled beyond endurance. In his frantic efforts to control himself, he upset the cup of tea he was handing to Muriel.

"What carelessness!" said Elaine, as she poured out another. "Now as a punishment for that, sir, *you* shall not go and see the orchids, but come a solemn walk with me in my own particular garden, where grow no rare and wonderful plants with long Latin names, but only sweet old-fashioned English flowers."

"Please may I come too?" asked Muriel wistfully.

"No, my dear! You are going to show Mr. Branscome the orchids."

*   *   *   *   *

Lady Elaine lay back in her chair, laughing in genuine amusement.

Guy, who ten minutes before had felt such an irresistible desire to laugh, now looked grave, and not altogether pleased.

"Look at them, Guy! Do you think they are anathematizing the orchids, and wishing me at the bottom of the sea; or do they feel properly grateful? Just see how they are walking across the lawn—as far apart as politeness will possibly admit. Silly people! There—now Mr. Branscome has widened the gap by at least three inches, and Muriel, not to be outdone, has made it six. Look!"

But Guy did not turn his head.

"You should not have put my friend into such a hole just now, Lady Elaine. It was very hard, both on him and on Miss Bruce."

"Oh! nonsense, my dear boy. They must be put into holes, as you call it. Don't you see that they are dying of love for each other, and only want someone to make them understand it? I shall soon bring matters to a crisis, if only you don't interfere and look so stern and indignant at me, when I am acting solely for their good. Now see! Muriel has dropped her parasol; I wonder if that was done on purpose? Anyway she has had to pick it up for herself. Now, if it had belonged to any other girl in the kingdom, Mr. Branscome would have had his wits about him, and picked it up for her at once; which proves nothing to your masculine mind, but, from a woman's point of view, most unanswerably proves that she is still 'par excellence,' *the* one girl in the kingdom to him, apart from all others. Now they are coming to the little gate. Just watch how they will go through; not like two ordinary mortals, or I am much mistaken. No! See! Both tried to pass through at once, and as the gate is very narrow, collided, and nearly got jammed there; then both retreated horrified, and apologised, without looking at each other; and both straightway went at it again! And, finally, Mr. Branscome has gone through *first*, leaving Muriel to follow. Now, confess, Guy: did you ever before know your friend be so *gauche* as to go through a gate, or door, or any aperture whatever, right in front of a lady?"

"I don't think I ever did," said Guy, laughing in spite of himself.

"Well, there you have it once more," went on Elaine, with an oracular wave of her hand. "According to feminine logic, that proves him to have been thinking more of *her* than of the gate, his manners, or anything else whatsoever. Ah! some day they will thank me for putting them 'in a hole,' when your friend has found his own heart again, and my sweet little Muriel has forgiven him his desertion, as she is certain to be foolish enough to do."

"Indeed, Lady Elaine," Guy said hotly, "Miss Bruce has nothing to forgive Cyril Branscome; rather, she has cause to ask his forgiveness."

Lady Elaine turned her head, and regarded him, through her half-closed lashes, with an amused, languid smile.

"My dear boy, there is really no occasion to look pitchforks at me over other people's quarrels. *You* have heard *his* version, so of course *you* say *he* is right; *I* have heard *her* version, so of course *I* say *she* is right. The fact is, both are right, and both are wrong; and it is really too hot for us to excite ourselves over the matter. You don't understand this sort of thing yet. Ah! by the way, though," she cried, with suddenly awakened interest, "that reminds me you have a love-story to tell me this afternoon. How came I so nearly to forget! Now, if you will excuse me for a few moments, I have some orders to give in the house; then we will go to my garden. Wait here. I shall not be long."

She rose, and as she passed him, Guy hastened to move a chair which stood in her way. Then she turned, and held up her finger at him laughingly.

"Ah ha, Sir Guy! Now, according to our feminine logic, *you* think more of your manners than of *me!*"

She passed on.

With his hand still resting on the back of the chair, Guy stood looking after her. His eyes followed her tall, graceful figure, as she swept across the lawn, her gown trailing noiselessly behind her. She had left her hat under the tree, and the slanting rays of the sun shone on her head, playing with her golden hair till it gleamed and glistened like a halo of light.

What is Guy thinking as he stands looking after her, with that sad wistful look on his face?

He saw her pause at her favourite rose-tree, and gather a handful of yellow blossoms, then pass through the open window and enter the house.

"How changed she is," Guy thought to himself; "how different to what I remember a year ago. Yesterday she seemed just the same as ever; but to-day so different. And yet, it would be hard to say exactly how.

But she used not to laugh so loud, or talk so fast, or say 'my dear boy' in that odd way to me. This is only the second time we have met since that miserable day; if she were not changed she never would have made that last remark. And yet, just when she is laughing most, such an awfully sad look comes over her face; and she ridicules everything so bitterly, as though nothing in this world were worth caring for, or thinking seriously about. I wonder what her life has been through this long year. And now—O my Lord, how shall I tell her!"

Guy ceased talking to himself, and looking up silently through the dark cedar boughs, spoke long and earnestly with Another.

CHAPTER XXII.

"We must make haste," said Lady Elaine; "or the lovers will be back, and we shall lose our *tête-à-tête*. I know Muriel will conscientiously show him every plant in the houses, and tell him all their names; but if they talk of nothing else, and stop for nothing by the way, that will not take very long. Do you see this high privet-hedge? Well, it goes all round my garden, and the only entrance is through this little archway, under the climbing rose. Please bend your head as you go under, or you will bring down some of my roses. I like them to hang in clusters from the top, though I have no doubt the gardeners think it most untidy; but here no gardener cuts a flower without my express orders. Now, what do you think of my garden?"

Guy looked around him with undisguised admiration. On either side of the smooth gravel walks, the long broad borders were brilliant with colour and bloom. Hollyhocks, tiger-lilies, pink and white foxgloves, purple irises, all raised their tall, graceful heads, and nodded them gently in the breeze, as if conscious that here their proud beauty was acknowledged, and triumphed over rarer, choicer flowers. Sweet peas, gladioli, carnations, all grew in abundance, a perfect blaze of colour and beauty; while here and there, in striking contrast, a great snow-white lily reared its tall head, and shone like a star amongst all the other flowers. Even the old-fashioned lavender and rosemary had their place, and the air was scented with sweet-briar. They grew in wild beauty and profusion, and yet were arranged and grouped with the most perfect taste. The gravel walks, neatly edged with box, all led to the centre of the garden, where a fountain played into a large marble basin, full of gold fish and water-lilies.

"I see you like it," said Lady Elaine, with a pleased smile.

"Like it!" cried Guy. "Rather! Did you arrange and plan it all?"

"Yes, entirely; and I think I know and love every single flower here. Did you notice how the fountain began to play the instant we entered the garden? That was an idea of my own. The key is in the arch, hidden amongst the roses. As I pass through I turn it, and start the fountain playing. It seems to burst up in welcome when I come into my garden; and I try to forget it is my own doing. It is so pleasant to be welcomed somewhere, sometimes. Come, Guy, we will walk all round, and up and down. You shall see my garden thoroughly."

"How the fountain sparkles and glitters,"

remarked Guy as they passed it; "and I do like the sound of falling water. It reminds me of Switzerland."

"Ah! there is that particular look, Guy. Switzerland? Does *she* live in Switzerland? or did you meet her in Switzerland? or what? Come, tell me all about it."

"Yes, I will; I will tell you all about it." Yet he paused, and looked straight before him, over the privet-hedge, over the tops of the scarlet horse-chestnuts beyond, away to where the little fleecy clouds were flecking the deep blue sky.

"Well, Guy? I am listening. Is it something so very difficult to tell?"

Then he turned impulsively, took both her hands in his for a moment, and looked into her face.

"It *is* rather difficult to tell," he said, "for two reasons. First: because I have so often thought of the time when I should be able to tell you this; that now it has come, it seems almost like a dream. Secondly: because you quite misunderstood what I meant yesterday in the wood. It is no woman's love, this which has come to me, and made me one of the happiest fellows living. It is no earthly love. It is something different altogether."

"What is it, then?" she asked wonderingly.

"It is the love of Christ, my Lord, who loved me, and gave Himself for me. Dear Lady Elaine, I can't put it eloquently, as it ought to be put; I can't express in words one half of what I mean. I can only just tell you simply, that since this time last year I have got to know Him—Jesus—as my own Saviour. I gave myself to Him, and He took me just as I was—a precious good-for-nothing fellow, as you know—but He took me, and He will keep me, and I am His for evermore."

Guy looked away again up to the deep blue sky. "*And I am His for evermore!*" he repeated, with a joyous ring in his voice, of perfect assurance, complete triumphant peace, which made it vibrate like the sweet low notes of a violin. Telling her had been an effort, a greater effort than he had expected ; but, in the telling, it had all come to him with tenfold more reality. Never before has he so clearly realized the fact that he is his Lord's ; for time, for eternity, *for ever*. At the moment he forgot all else.

Lady Elaine's voice, speaking in tones of intense astonishment, recalled him to earth.

"Indeed! Then you have become *religious*, Guy?"

"No," he said earnestly. "No, not religious in the sense you mean; in the sense we sometimes used to talk about religion, and religious people. In that sense, religion is the equivalent for unreality; religious people, for humbugs. That is why I always made up my mind, come what might, I would never be religious. But this,—oh! this is quite different. The great thing about it is, that it is all a reality. *He* is a Reality; forgiveness, rest, peace, are all realities; not canting phrases or figures of speech. And the happiness He gives is real, too. You know how wretched I was when I went away; but, oh! I wish you knew how happy I am now. Do you think I am a humbug, Lady Elaine?"

He turned to her; his face was shining.

She looked at him searchingly, hesitatingly. Guy broke into a joyous laugh.

"Why, Lady Elaine, I really believe you do!"

"Of course not, Guy; but I don't understand; I can't think what you mean. Do you read the Prayer-Book every day of the week, and say the Psalms, and all that sort of thing? I am very glad you are happy—for I see you *are* happy. I saw that in your face in church, even before I had talked to you at all. But, oh, Guy! why couldn't you be happy without taking up these strange ideas?

It makes you seem such a long way off. I don't understand anything about it, and I hate mysteries; I always did."

Her voice quivered, and she turned away her head; but not before Guy had seen the tears in her eyes. This was so entirely different to what he had expected. He had thought she would laugh at him a bit at first, and then let him tell her all about it. But this? Guy did not know what to make of it; and the sight of tears in those sweet eyes made him feel—well, queer.

They walked a little way in silence. Then Guy said gently—almost tenderly, it seemed to her, being so little used to sympathy:

"May I tell you all about it, Lady Elaine, right from the beginning? You will see then that there is no mystery; it is so simple and clear. And I found it all, every word—where do you think? Why, in your own little Bible."

"In my Bible?" Lady Elaine's astonishment increased. "I am sure there is nothing of the kind there."

"Ah, but there is!" said Guy. "Look, here it is. But you must not ask for it back. I could never part with it now."

He took her little Bible from his pocket, and placed it in her hands. Lady Elaine examined it curiously. It was worn, and had evidently been much used. As she opened it and turned over the leaves many marked passages caught her eye, and notes scribbled on the margin here and there. She turned to the fly-leaf. It was her lost Bible, undoubtedly; her name was there in her own handwriting: "*Elaine, Oct. 8th.*" Underneath this, in Guy's, was the date of that June evening when she met him in the woods, and the text he had marked in the Bible he then sent her: "*Many waters cannot quench love, neither can the floods drown it,*" but a firm dark line had been drawn through this, and beneath another and a later date, these words were written:

"His *love to me was wonderful.*"
"*He loved me, and gave Himself for me.*"

Lady Elaine looked at Guy. He had turned away, and was examining one of her white lilies. Then she looked again at the words he had obliterated, and at those beneath; and somehow she began to understand.

"Guy," she said, "come here."

He came, and stood beside her. She looked at him and smiled. Then pointed to the open page.

"Guy, am I to erase the pencil marks under those words in the Bible you sent me?"

Guy flushed painfully.

"Please do," he said.

"But I don't think I shall," she went on; looking at him with a half amused smile. "It is one of my favourite texts."

"Lady Elaine," Guy said, speaking very low, with evident effort, and without raising his eyes from the ground; "I see you have forgiven, but I want you quite to forget what happened on that miserable day. I can never regret it enough. If only I had known then what I know now—if only I had been then as I am now—it could never, never have happened."

"Why not?" she asked lightly, half laughing.

"Because," said Guy, "the Master I am now trying to serve not only grants forgiveness, but also gives the power to overcome all *sin*."

He looked up as he spoke, and beneath his earnest eyes the smile in hers died away. She shut the book, and gave it him back.

"Well, Guy, tell me all about it; but don't expect me to understand, for I never can comprehend spiritual mysteries; and to become really good, and quite religious, would not be at all in my line. But don't look so discouraged; if anyone ever *converts* me—that is the word, is it not?—I promise it shall be you! Let us come up on to the terrace at the end here, where we can walk up and down, and see the sunset over the hedge. Now tell me what first put these queer ideas into your head."

Perhaps this preface hardly made it more easy; but truly Guy was what Paul calls "a good soldier of Jesus Christ," and not easily daunted, even by a woman's smile, sometimes the hardest of all things to face.

In his simple, straightforward way he told her from the beginning, just as he had told Cyril on that September evening in the Swiss pension. And as she listened her face softened into real interest; she dropped the expression of mock gravity she had at first assumed, and the sweet eyes raised to his were full of sympathy and earnest attention. Lady Elaine could understand the yearnings of a tired heart after rest; the anxious seeking of a soul after something which would really satisfy, and not end, like all else, in disappointment. She herself had often vaguely sought she knew not what—and sought in vain; and now Guy had sought, and seemed to think he had found.

Half an hour later, when Muriel looked in through the rose-covered arch, they were still walking slowly up and down the grassy terrace at the bottom of Elaine's garden, Guy's head bent down towards her as if talking very earnestly. They did not see Muriel, and she, preoccupied with her own thoughts, was glad to slip away by herself. Cyril Branscome, after seeing the orchid house, had pleaded an engagement and taken his leave, requesting her to apologize to Lady Elaine, when they failed to find her on returning to the lawn.

* * * * *

"I understand what you mean, but I cannot see it, Guy. I cannot see that any of these promises are meant for *me*, individually. And even if they are, it all seems to want more imagination than I am capable of."

"It does not want imagination, Lady Elaine, but simple faith."

"Well, but how can we love One whom we do not know; or trust Him, either?"

"We cannot, until we know Him; but if we really seek Him, we find Him, and learn to know Him, oh, so well! One of His clearest promises is: 'They that seek Me shall find me,' and when we have found Him the question is not, how can we love Him; but, how could we possibly not love Him."

"One whom we have never seen."

"Yes," said Guy. "'Whom having not seen ye love; in whom, though now ye see Him not, yet believing ye rejoice with joy unspeakable and full of glory.' That is one of my favourite verses, for it exactly expresses what I have felt ever since I found Him."

Elaine looked into his face.

"Well," she said, with a weary sigh, "only one thing in the whole matter seems real to me at present; and that is *you*, Guy.

I can see in you the reflection of it all. I believe *you* believe, though I suppose that will not be of much use to me! Ah, well! Every heart knows its own burden. These sort of things never will be realities to me, I am afraid."

"Often at first," said Guy, "I lost the feeling of their being real. I knew it, but I could not realize it. One day I came across some lines, a sort of prayer. I have said them ever since, the first thing in the morning and the last thing at night. It has helped so much to keep it all clear and bright. May I tell them to you, and perhaps you will try it too?"

They had walked up the path to the fountain. Elaine sat down on the marble edge.

"It is no use telling me. I should never remember. Just write it down for me, Guy; here on my tablets will do."

She passed him her ivory tablets, and a

little gold, jewelled pencil-case. He put up one foot on the edge of the fountain, and wrote on his knee. Elaine dabbled her hand in the water the while, and dropped little bits of moss to the goldfish, who swam up expecting crumbs. Guy could not help seeing the entry at the top of the tablet. *To-day G. and friend at 4 to tea. Montague comes by the 6.30 train. To ball at Lord K.'s with Monty to-morrow night.*

Under this Guy wrote the words he had found so precious.

> " O Jesus, make Thyself to me
> A living, bright reality.
> More present to faith's vision keen
> Than any outward object seen.
> More dear, more intimately nigh,
> Than e'en the sweetest earthly tie."

He passed it to her silently. She read it through, half aloud. At the last line she paused. "'*Than e'en the sweetest earthly tie.*' The sweetest earthly tie! And how sweet do you suppose my earthly ties are?"

Then she burst out laughing.

Guy looked very troubled, but not exactly knowing how to answer, said nothing.

"I am afraid," she went on, laughing hysterically, "if this prayer were answered, and He were made as dear to me as *that*, I should not be much the better for it."

A spasm of pain passed over Guy's face. These words were very precious to him; and he thought she was speaking of them lightly. He could not understand that depth of misery, too bitter for anything so soothing as tears, which takes refuge in laughter. He held out his hand for the tablets.

"I had better rub it out again," he said coldly.

"You shall do nothing of the kind!" cried Elaine sharply; then with a half-sob: "How can you be so unkind to me, Guy?"

Poor Guy was entirely bewildered.

"I did not mean to be unkind," he said

gently; "but you seemed to think the words do not apply to you."

"Well, do they?" she asked, and laughed again.

"I cannot tell," said Guy gravely. "Have you never had a sweet earthly tie of any sort, Lady Elaine, which might give the words a real meaning for you?"

Suddenly, as he spoke, her expressive face changed again. A softened, tender look came over it: a look of yearning, wistful love. She answered very low, as if speaking more to herself than to him, and looked down into the water as she spoke:

"Yes—yes, I had once—very, very sweet it was—wonderfully sweet—the sweetest earthly tie! Once, long ago—I had forgotten—shall I tell you about it, Guy? Would you like to know?"

Guy was startled by her manner. She looked so strange, and he thought she spoke almost as though she were wandering in mind.

"Not now," he said hastily. "Some day, dear Lady Elaine, I should like to know, if you care to tell me; but now we have talked so long, and you are tired. Shall we go back to the house?"

She smiled quietly, and took her hand out of the water, letting the sparkling drops run from her fingers into a large water-lily. Then she dried her hand with her handkerchief, and turned to Guy.

"No, I am not tired; not more tired than usual. It is so cool and nice here now; pleasanter than in the house. What time is it? Just six? Well, I do not expect my husband and my cousin until after seven. Do stay, Guy, unless you want to go. What time do you dine?"

"Not before eight."

"Oh, don't hurry away, then. And apparently Muriel and Mr. Branscome are getting on very well without us. But this fountain makes such a noise, we can hardly hear ourselves speak. Will you go and stop it: you will find the key halfway up the arch on the left-hand side: it is quite covered by the roses."

It was some time before Guy could find it, and turn off the fountain. When he came back, Lady Elaine seemed quite herself again.

"Very few people know about it, Guy. Perhaps it is an odd story to tell to a young fellow like you, and you may not care to hear it; but I want you to know; and then, if ever you think me hard, and bitter and unforgiving, you will understand a little of what I have suffered, and will not judge me too harshly."

She paused, and looked at him for a moment, smiling sadly. Then she unfastened a chain she wore round her neck, and drew from under her dress a plain gold locket. As she did so she glanced around nervously, as if to make sure they were not observed.

Then she touched a spring. The locket flewopen. She looked at it silently for some moments, then handed it to Guy. He examined it curiously. Set round with magnificent diamonds, he saw a tiny curl of gold-brown hair. He looked up inquiringly at Lady Elaine.

"Whose is it?" he asked.

She bent forward, and answered him almost in a whisper:

"My little dead baby's!"

Guy gave a start of intense surprise.

"You did not know that I once had a little son, Guy?"

"No," he said; and looked at the small curl almost reverently; then gave it back to her in silence.

She took it from him and sat looking at it while she spoke—so low at first that Guy had to bend forward, to hear all she said.

"I had been married nearly eighteen months when my baby came. I did not want a baby, and I thought it a horrid nuisance. I was only eighteen myself—a child—not fit to be a mother. I don't think I loved it at all; though I knew people would call me unnatural if they knew. I had had a great deal of trouble, and my heart seemed dead and incapable of any feeling whatever. I was very weak and ill for a long time; and the baby drove me nearly wild if it cried in my room. 'Take it away, nurse,' I used to say; 'take it away this instant.' 'Does your ladyship really mean him to go? He will soon be quiet again.' 'Take it away, I tell you! I can't have a screaming child in my room.' 'Very well, my lady.' And she would take it up and go; and, as she left the room, I could hear her kissing it, and saying, 'A poor little dear; doesn't its mother want it then!' And I used to lie and think to myself: 'I don't want anyone, or anything, but to be at peace;' and I wished—oh, how I wished I were dead!"

She paused, and bending till her lips nearly touched the locket lying in her hand, murmured very low :

"My little pet; you have forgiven me now!

"When I was well again and downstairs as usual, I used to have the baby brought down every afternoon, to be with me for a little while. Not that I cared to have it, particularly; but I did not like the servants to talk, and say the child was neglected; and I felt I had done my duty, if I had it with me for ten minutes every day. While I was having my cup of afternoon tea the nurse would bring it in, lay it on my lap, and come for it again in a quarter of an hour. It was a quiet little thing, and if my book was an interesting one, I scarcely knew it was there.

"One afternoon, when it was about three months old, it had arrived for its little daily visit, and been lying in my lap some minutes, when I happened to glance down, and saw its deep blue eyes fixed on me, with such an earnest look in them. I put down my book and looked into its little face. It smiled back into mine. I took up my book again and tried to read; but all the while I was conscious of those soft little blue eyes watching me.

"The nurse came in, took it up, and carried it off. As she walked across the drawing-room, I saw it turn its little head in her arms to look after me as it went. Something in its eyes, Guy, went to my heart. Before she reached the door, I called to her: 'Nurse, you can bring the baby back for a few minutes.' 'Very well, my lady.' She looked surprised, but laid it on my knee again. 'You can come when I ring.'

"When she was gone, I bent down over it. 'My baby,' I said, 'my little baby, why do you look at me like that? Do you know I am your mother? Do you—do you love me?' He looked into my eyes and smiled—oh, such a smile!—and then stretched up his little arms to me; and as I bent over him, one of those little fat hands touched my cheek. Then I burst into tears, and wept as I had never been able to weep since I was a child at home. My baby seemed to think it was all for his amusement; for he lay laughing and cooing on my lap, though his little face was wet with my tears. Then such a wonderful joy dawned in my heart. He loved me: my little baby loved me; and he was quite my own; no one could take him from me. I could hardly believe it! Really at last to have someone to love me; and he my own little son! I kissed his little mouth, and asked him over and over again: 'My baby, are you *sure* you love me? Do you really know I am your mother?' I was wearing a gold locket set with stones, and a sudden fear came over me lest it was the glitter of these which attracted him. I slipped it off and hid it away; but he smiled and laughed at me just the same. I wept again for joy. 'Oh, my darling, my little one.' I whispered; 'I love you, I love you; and you love me; and we belong to each other; no one in this big world can part us; and some day those sweet little lips will call me *mother.*' Then I bent over him, and covered him with kisses.

"I carried him upstairs myself, and sat by, watching the nurses undress him. I remember their faces of astonishment when I knelt down on the floor and kissed his little pink toes. I could hardly sleep that night, for thinking of my little boy. I got up two or three times and stole into the nursery, to make sure he was quite safe and sleeping soundly in his bassinette.

"From that day he was my great delight. I gave up nearly all my time to him. I learnt to wash and dress him myself. I knitted his little socks, and opened my long-closed piano to play to him when he came downstairs. I was so happy; for my baby loved me, and I loved him—Oh! God knows how I loved him."

She paused, and took a long look at the little curl; then closed the locket, and held it tightly clenched in her hand.

"My husband was in Parliament at that time. He wished to go to London for part of the season, when my baby was just six months old. He took a house; then informed me of the arrangement, and that I must be ready to go with him by the end of the week. 'But I cannot take baby to London,' I said; 'especially in this weather.' 'Certainly not. I do not intend you should.' 'But I cannot leave him!' I cried, my heart standing still at the thought; 'and what is more, I *will not* leave him.' My husband is a man of few words. 'You will come to London with me,' he said, 'and your child will remain here. He has two nurses to see to him, and does not require you. I will have no nonsense. I expect you to be ready on Friday.'

"I was ready on Friday. I left my little baby; although the nurse was a new one, who had only been with us a fortnight. I left him—and for two long months I was away from him in London. Oh, how I missed him! How sick at heart I grew with longing for him; especially in the evening, at his bed-time, when I used to undress him, and play with him, and sing him to sleep in my arms!

"At last we returned home. The instant we arrived I flew to the nursery. In another moment my boy was in my arms! My boy? I scarcely knew him! The thin, worn little face, drawn with a look of pain; the large bright eyes, with dark circles beneath them. Was this my lovely boy! the beautiful baby I had left?

"'What is the matter with him?' I cried, turning sharply to the nurse. She looked astonished, and said he was quite well; nothing was the matter. I called a servant who was passing. 'Run down quickly,' I said, 'and tell one of the men to go for the doctor as fast as horse can take him.'

"Oh! my baby, my baby! He lay in my arms so quiet and still. His sweet little smile was the only thing unchanged. I kissed him and held him tight, and tried to hope; but, oh! Guy, from the first moment I saw him, I knew—I knew he was dying.

"He was ill for several weeks. The doctors said neglect in his feeding had started the illness; and with all their skill they could not arrest it: they were sent for too late. We got a trained nurse; but I scarcely left him night or day. My husband seemed sorry at first, though he declared it would have happened just the same if I had been at home; but after awhile he became annoyed at my grief and anxiety, and insisted on my dressing and coming to dinner every evening, whether my baby was better or worse. I dared not disobey him.

"At last, one evening while I was dressing, the under-nurse tapped at my door. ' Please come to the nursery, my lady. Baby is not so well.' I hurriedly finished my toilet, and went. The nurse had seen a change approaching, and told me so. 'Oh nurse!' I said, 'give him to me. If my little baby must die, let him die in my arms.' 'Poor lady!' she said, and gently laid him there.

"I don't know how long I sat looking into that little white face. Suddenly a heavy tread in the room startled me. My husband stood before me. 'Elaine!' he said harshly, and at the sound of his voice the little face at my breast quivered with pain. 'What does this mean? Dinner has been waiting twenty minutes. I have sent up for you twice.' The nurse came forward. 'I stopped the footman at the door, sir. Her ladyship cannot come down. The baby is——' She whispered the last word, that I might not hear it. 'Nonsense, woman!' said my husband angrily. 'This baby has been supposed to be dying for the last three weeks. Come to dinner, Elaine.' 'Oh, no, no!' I cried, 'I cannot leave him! I can't leave my baby!' He came a step nearer. 'Take the child, nurse,' he said. Then I rose, and put him into her arms. She was a good woman. Her eyes were full of tears. 'Promise to send at once for me if he seems any worse,' I whispered. 'Keep up heart, dear lady,' she answered. 'I will send if there is the slightest change.' My husband took my arm and led me to the dining-room.

"During dinner he happened to leave the room. As he came back, I heard him speaking to someone in the ante-room. Ten minutes later the footman came in, and silently laid down a slip of paper on the table beside him. He glanced at it, and changed colour. Then he rose, and came round to where I sat. He looked scared and startled. 'Elaine,' he said, 'you may go to the nursery now; but finish your wine first.' I drank it hastily, and ran upstairs. I heard him following behind me. As I entered the room, the nurse rushed forward. Baby was not in her arms. 'Stay, my lady! Wait one minute! Sir, does she know?' I pushed past her to the bed, where that little motionless figure lay.

"My little baby was dead, and he had not died in my arms.

"I could not weep. I could only stand and look at him. Then I turned upon the nurse. 'Why did you not send for me?' I cried. 'I did send,' she said. 'Jane went down quite a quarter of an hour ago.' 'Jane!' She came forward. 'I met my master in the ante-room, and told him, my lady.' I turned and faced him. I think I was half mad with anguish. 'What!' I cried. 'you knew; and let me sit on at dinner, while my baby died!'—'Be silent, Elaine,' he said. 'Don't forget yourself before servants. I am sorry for your trouble; but I will not have you make such a fuss about nothing.' 'About nothing!' I cried. 'You call it *nothing*, that all the joy has gone out of my life for evermore. I loved my little baby, and he loved me. How dare you sneer! He *did* love me. You brute! I wish with all my heart that you lay there, as he does; though I know your wicked soul would not be where my little angel's is now.' 'Oh, my lady, my lady!' cried the nurse, coming between us. I pushed her away. 'Which is as much as to say,' said my husband, with a rough laugh, 'that you wish me dead and damned!' 'I do,' I said; 'for you have killed my baby! If I had not left him, he would never have been ill. You made me go; so you have killed him!' I think I was almost mad. 'Look here!' he said, speaking in tones of suppressed rage, which, at any other time, would have made me tremble. 'This is all very fine, madam, and will make nice talk in the servants' hall, if that is what you want. But I remember once hearing you say: "I wish that squalling brat had never been born."' 'Sir, how can you!' exclaimed the nurse indignantly. I came close up to him. 'Listen!' I said calmly; 'I never loved you, *as you know.* Now I hate you; I will never, never forgive you, so long as I live—never—*never*—NEVER!' He raised his arm, as if to fell me to the ground. I saw the nurse catch hold of it, and I remember no more; for I sank fainting on the bed where my little dead child lay.

"When I returned to life and reason, after the long illness that followed, the little grave in the churchyard was growing green. The nurseries had been entirely refurnished; the bassinette, the little clothes, the baby-toys—all, all had been sent away—I needed not to ask by whose orders—and the last ten months appeared to me a sweet, sad, awful dream. I often longed for one tiny little sock to weep over—one little worn blue shoe to kiss—so that at least I could have felt certain that I had really been a mother.

"But before my good nurse left me she slipped into my hand a carefully-folded packet. 'I thought your ladyship would wish for this,' she said, 'and I cut it off, myself, as he lay in his little coffin, when nobody was by.' When I opened the many wrappings of silver paper, I found one little gold-brown curl. It was all that was left me of my baby-boy."

Lady Elaine ceased speaking, and hid her face in her hands.

Presently she looked up with a sad smile, and held out her hand to Guy.

"Don't look so sad, dear boy. Perhaps I ought not to have told you all this. No one else knows it. But you will keep my secret ; and you will not judge me harshly for not being so good as I might be. Troubles like these make one grow very hard and reckless. Do you understand ?"

Guy never could remember what he said then. But he knew that he held her thin white hand tight in his two big strong ones, and tried to make her understand what he felt about her terrible trouble ; and he knew that he broke down when he began to speak, and the foxgloves, and hollyhocks, and lilies, all began to swim in one confused blur of colour ; and he had to dash his sleeve across his eyes, and bolt out of the garden.

※ ※ ※ ※ ※

"Here is Mr. Monk," said Lady Elaine, as they strolled back to the house ; "and my cousin is with him."

Guy looked at the two men coming towards them. Full well he remembered that short, thickset figure and large massive head, with bushy black beard and eyebrows.

But who was this tall, handsome man, walking beside him, whose dark eyes flashed as he saw them coming, and who called out playfully:

"Hullo, Elaine!"

"Do stay a few minutes," said Lady Elaine. "This is my cousin—Lord Montague Errol."

CHAPTER XXIII.

A CLOUD of dust on the high road. The sound of horse's hoofs approaching at a quick gallop. Guy Mervyn turned the corner, mounted on his favourite horse, riding in hot haste, Bidger scudding along like the wind in front of him. It was a peculiarity of Bidger's always to go before, where the generality of dogs follow after.

The whole turn-out, as it dashed into view, flurried and startled a stout old lady, who, beneath the shelter of a huge scarlet parasol, was peacefully taking her walks abroad.

She was perfectly safe on the raised footpath at the side of the road; nevertheless she stood still, and held on to a post with her disengaged hand, while horse and dog swept by her. But suddenly recognising Guy Mervyn in the rider, she frantically waved her red parasol, and hailed him as she might have done a passing omnibus. Guy reined in his horse with dangerous rapidity; and, swerving round, drew up beside her, and laughingly raised his hat.

"My—dear—Sir Guy! What a terrible way to ride; and what a perfectly awful way to stop!"

"My dear Mrs. Joram, what else can you expect if you hail a fellow who is riding seven miles to an important appointment, for which he is already a quarter of an hour late!"

"Which means, I suppose, that I am not to detain you?"

"No, no," said Guy, springing off on to the footpath, and slipping the reins over his arm. "As I am late already, I may just as well be later. Besides, then I can screen myself behind you for the whole of my wrong-doing. My mother and the girls are shopping in Grayley, and I was to meet them at the photographer's at two o'clock. They have persuaded me to undergo the ordeal, and I am to do so beneath their auspices this afternoon. Beryl is wild about it, and has definitely settled upon at least a dozen attitudes in which I am to be done: a wonderful variety, I assure you; easy, nonchalant, graceful, martial, tragic, comic. I don't know what will be the outcome!"

"At any rate," said Mrs. Joram, as they walked on; "you must promise me one."

"Certainly, if they come to anything, and you are so good as to wish for one."

"Now, Sir Guy, I won't keep you a minute, but I must just ask you: Is it really the case, as they say in the village, that you are going to have a *meeting* on Sunday evening, under the trees in the park; an open-air meeting, to which anyone who likes may come?"

"Really, I am," said Guy, smiling. "Unlike most village rumours, it is perfectly true."

"But, my dear Sir Guy—what a very curious thing! I hope it is not going to be Revivalism, or the Salvation Army, or Moody and Sankey, or any of those sort of proceedings which go on in the open air, and often lead, I believe, to shocking results; really *shocking!*"

"Don't be alarmed, Mrs. Joram. It is only going to be me."

"You! But, my dear Sir Guy, what is to take place?"

"Would you like to see my invitation to our villagers? You must understand, it is only meant for them."

Guy felt in his pocket, and produced a folded paper. "I have sent one of these to all our cottages."

Mrs. Joram handed him her parasol to hold; got out her glasses, and put them on; then stood still in the middle of the path, and read Guy's letter aloud, very emphatically, with little approving nods at every comma, and a running commentary between.

"'Mervyn Hall.

"'My dear Friends,'—

"(Ah! yes, I like that. You landowners should always be friendly and conciliatory towards the lower classes; calling them dear friends may possibly make them so; at least, if anything can, which I consider a doubtful point)—'I am glad to be once more at home amongst you, after my long absence abroad. I shall hope soon to see you all personally, and hear how you have been getting on while I have been away.' (Poor dear Sir Guy! To what an amount of grumbling you will have to listen!) 'Meanwhile, I want you all—or as many of you as can—to meet me under the great oak in the park next Sunday evening, at half-past six o'clock. I have something to tell you, my friends, which I have found out during my travels. I want you all to know about it, for it is something well worth knowing. Perhaps to some of you it will not be new; but to others it may. This time last year it would have been news to me; and as it is real good news, now I know it, I do not wish to keep it to myself. Come if you can on Sunday, and I will tell you all about it.

"' Believe me to be

"' Your friend and well-wisher,

"' GUY MERVYN.'

"Well, now really, Sir Guy"—old Mrs. Joram's eyes twinkled—"it is very clever of you to give them no sort of idea what it is all to be about, and yet say sufficient to excite their curiosity. There is nothing like curiosity for bringing people out. You will have all the village there! And that is a clever hint, that perhaps some of them know it already. They will each want to prove that they knew, and their neighbours didn't; do all will take care to be there. But now, really, what is it to be about? Why, it might be a lecture on Switzerland, or other foreign parts; or it might" — Mrs. Joram chuckled, and held up her finger at him—" it might even be a faithful description of the argillo-calcareous mud at the bottom of the Lake of Geneva! Eh, Sir Guy?"

Guy, who had entirely forgotten his guide-book letter, looked at the old lady as if he suspected her of having suddenly taken leave of her senses.

" But seriously, my dear," she went on, laying her hand on his coat-sleeve, and looking up into his face, " is it what you told me about the other day, when we were talking over Church matters, and other similar topics?"

"Yes, Mrs. Joram, it is."

"Now, *really!* Then it *is* to be a species of religious gathering, and *you* will deliver the sermon. Do you remember that Sunday long ago, when you and I and Lady Elaine walked to church together, and you declared, if you had the arranging of things, all the congregation should adjourn to the woods, and have the service under some shady tree; and I said I should like to hear what sort of a sermon you would give them? We little thought it would ever come so nearly true. Will Mr. Drawler be there?"

"Jupiter Ammon! I hope not!" cried Guy, in his dismay letting one of his old boyish expressions slip out.

"Oh, hush!" said Mrs. Joram, pretending to be greatly shocked. "My dear Sir Guy, you really must not invoke heathen deities. Pray, don't do that on Sunday evening! But do invite Mr. Drawler."

"Not if I know it," said Guy.

"Oh, but *do!* It is not that I have any special partiality for him, myself. But you see he *is* our Vicar, and his presence will lend an air of orthodoxy to the whole proceeding. Otherwise some unpleasant people may spread a rumour that the master of Mervyn Hall has a leaning towards Dissent."

"Well," said Guy, laughing, "I am afraid I must accept that appalling alternative. Of course, I could not exclude Mr. Drawler if he chooses to come; but I devoutly hope he will not do so, and I most certainly shall not invite him. It is simply and solely for the poor—my own tenants."

"Well, then, *I* am included, at all events, seeing that Rookwood is in the Mervyn property. Why! I really believe you did not know it! It is a good thing you have such a paragon of a steward to manage your business matters for you. But I see Bidger is exercised in his mind as to this appointment at the photographer's. Look how he keeps starting off in haste, then trotting back with reproving looks at me. Good, intelligent old dog! You should have his likeness taken also."

"That is in the programme. One of Berry's proposed attitudes is for me to stand with one hand on Bidger's head, the other extended as if setting him on at something. The only drawback is, that I am afraid Bidger would promptly spring upon the photographer, and demolish the camera!"

"Oh, no! Not if you explain that you are only posing. He is so remarkably intelligent. Understands rather *too* much, I think, sometimes. He made great friends with Elaine while you were away. I believe he used constantly to pay her little private calls on his own account. I know for a fact that he was lying at her feet in the garden the whole of one afternoon. I saw it myself. She was using his great shaggy back as a footstool."

"He was quite right," said Guy. "I always teach him to be civil to all my friends."

"Well, he never called on *me!*" remarked Mrs. Joram archly. "However, I suppose Bidger prefers the young and the beautiful! Well, now, I really must not keep you any longer. Good-bye, Sir Guy. And I may come on Sunday?"

"Certainly, if you like. But don't expect a sermon. And look here! You mustn't laugh at me, dear old friend; for it is not an easy thing to do. It really will be rather an ordeal."

"Bless you, my dear!" she answered, patting his arm, and looking kindly into his face. "I would not laugh at you for worlds. I like having my little jokes with people I care about—that is all. Only, mind you keep in the old paths, and be a true son of the Church."

"Talking of old paths," said Guy, "I think I have settled old Bones for you. I saw Mr. Drawler the day after we talked it over, and he is quite willing to dispense with Bones, and have the new arrangement, provided I pay the extra money, and also undertake to make Bones quite happy about the change. I told him we really could not stand the pelican last Sunday, but he seemed to see nothing either funny or objectionable in Bones announcing to the whole congregation in his stentorian tones: 'I ham become like a peeley-can in the wilderness, and a howl in the desert.' However, he consents, which is the chief thing; and I have no doubt I shall easily square old Bones. So we have succeeded with our first improvement. Well, good-bye."

Guy vaulted into the saddle, and was soon out of sight.

Mrs. Joram went on her way, every now and then smiling to herself complacently.

Presently she overtook Lady Elaine, or rather, met her at the cross-roads.

"Well, Elaine. I have just been talking to Guy Mervyn. Have you seen him to speak to, since his return? He is perfectly charming."

"Yes." said Elaine. "He and Mr. Branscome came to tea with us yesterday afternoon."

"Well, is he not charming? And he has come back quite a young St. Augustine—full of delightful new ideas. Did he talk to you about them?"

"What sort of ideas do you mean?" inquired Lady Elaine.

"Oh! I really can't explain, if you don't know; but I dare say he will tell you himself some day. He might not have said anything to me about it—though he always *did* talk very freely to me—but we were discussing Church matters, and so it came out that he thinks more of such things than he used to do."

"Indeed?" said Lady Elaine. "Of Church matters?"

"You seem incredulous," retorted Mrs. Joram, in her little quick, impatient way. "Nevertheless, it is true. He is quite *earnest;* as I say, just my idea of St. Augustine in his youth. I wonder at your looking amused, Elaine; I really do. You and Sir Guy used to be great friends. I should have thought you would be pleased to hear this of him."

"Oh, I am not amused," said Elaine, putting on her languid manner, which always particularly annoyed Mrs. Joram. "Not at all. I see nothing amusing in being like St. Augustine. I always considered him a really horrid old person."

Mrs. Joram became nearly as scarlet as her parasol.

"Really, Lady Elaine, you ought to know better than to speak so of one of the Fathers of the Church! I am ashamed, perfectly ashamed, to hear it! Pray, do not make that sort of remark to Sir Guy."

"Oh, he and I do not discuss Church matters," said Elaine, with a slight tinge of sarcasm in her tone.

"Well," remarked Mrs. Joram presently, "I do not think he would mind my telling you about his meeting. Next Sunday evening all the villagers are to gather under the great oak in the park, and he himself is going to talk to them about religion. He is evidently very anxious to raise their tone and make them more earnest—so like St. Augustine again. He has had a letter printed and sent round to them all."

Mrs. Joram fumbled in her pocket and produced it, with a side glance at Elaine, hoping to see some signs of curiosity in her face. None being apparent, she opened the paper, but still retained it in her hand.

"I am not quite sure," she said doubtfully, "whether I ought to show it you. Sir Guy might not——"

"Never mind about showing it me," said

Elaine innocently. "He gave me one himself, yesterday."

This was the snub direct, and rather hard on poor little Mrs. Joram, so full of importance over being in Guy's confidence; but then she had succeeded in 'riling' Lady Elaine, and Lady Elaine disliked being 'riled.'

Mrs. Joram soon found an excuse to march on in double-quick time.

Elaine sat on a stile to rest, and watched the old lady's retreating figure, thinking how very much that parasol resembled a huge red toadstool.

Presently she burst out laughing.

"He like St. Augustine!" she said. "What next, I wonder!"

CHAPTER XXIV.

THE long drive to and from Grayley, and the afternoon of shopping, had tired Mrs. Mervyn. She did not stay in the garden for the hour of chatter and fun which invariably followed five o'clock tea at Mervyn Hall, but went to her boudoir to rest.

Lying on a couch near the open window, she could hear the birds singing their evening hymn, and watch the lovely sunset tints. Occasionally she laid down her knitting and smiled, as Guy's voice reached her from the garden, or Berry's merry little laugh pealed out, and came rippling in at the window, like the song of a bird.

The sun went down, the twilight deepened,

the sound of voices in the garden ceased; and Guy's mother lay there alone, in the deep stillness of the summer evening.

There are lines of anxious thought upon her face. Such a kind, sweet face it is; shaded with soft brown hair, streaked here and there with silver ; essentially a mother's face, with that gentle smile, and those tender anxious eyes. More than one young motherless heart, meeting with Mrs. Mervyn, had leapt up and half said " Mother !" and none needed to fear a rebuff who sought kindness and love from her. Just now, as she lay watching the golden glory slowly fading in the sky, her mind was evidently preoccupied with anxious and somewhat perplexing thoughts. She sighed once or twice, and murmured half aloud : " Dear boy !"

Presently the door opened gently, and Guy came in.

" Mother darling ! lying all alone in the twilight ?" He kicked a footstool close up to the sofa. "Now for a quiet little spoon all to ourselves," he said.

She drew his head down to her breast, and kissed his forehead tenderly.

"My sweet one, I was just thinking of you."

"You mustn't look sad when you think of me, mother. What was it about?"

She stroked his hair gently for a minute before she answered.

"I cannot help feeling rather anxious about you just now, dear boy. I do so long to shield you from all harm, from everything that could bring any sorrow or trouble upon you; just as I did when you were a little fellow, quite under your mother's wing. I feel so powerless to do it now, as I did then; and yet the yearning to be able is stronger than ever."

She sighed; she knew he could not understand. Who but a mother could?

Guy drew down her hand and kissed it;

then held it close in a strong, loving clasp. How he loved her—this dear little mother of his, so dependent on him in many ways, and yet so anxious to settle and arrange all that concerned him.

"You see, my darling," she went on, "of course I know you are quite old enough now to go where you please, and choose your own acquaintances. I cannot expect you to be guided by me as to where you should visit; or to give up a friend at my desire. I should not ask it of you, Guy dear. I like my son to grow up and judge for himself in these matters. But I have felt a little troubled lately. I do not like to say more, lest you should misunderstand me."

Guy raised his head, and, though the twilight was deepening fast, she could see the look of love shining in his eyes.

"We never misunderstand each other, mother—you and I," he said simply.

She smoothed the wavy hair back from his forehead and gazed into his face.

"Oh, Guy, my son, what a joy you are to your mother!" She drew his head down again. "I have not forgotten, darling, what you told me when we talked over your renewing a certain acquaintance. I quite understood all you meant then, and I think I felt you were right; but now that the time has come, I begin to have such misgivings, Guy. Suppose your theory fails you?"

"It is not theory, mother; it is fact. I knew I should be kept; I know I shall be kept—'kept by the power of God.'"

"But, Guy dear, Scripture says 'the heart is deceitful above all things.'"

"Yes," said Guy; "but it also says: 'God is greater than our heart and knoweth all things'; and this is the promise I depend on most: 'He is able to keep you from falling.' Besides, remember, mother, I have given my heart to Him, and 'I know whom I have believed, and am persuaded that *He is able to keep* that which I have committed unto Him!'"

Mrs. Mervyn sighed, and looked perplexed.

"My dear boy, you have such a way of applying Scripture just to your own special needs. It makes it exceedingly difficult to differ from you without appearing to contradict God's word, which, of course, one would never dream of doing. I think all these passages only bear a general interpretation; you should not build too much upon them."

Guy smiled, but did not answer.

His mother went on:

"I know so much more of the world and the world's ways than you do, my son; and I can see quagmires and quicksands which you never suspect."

Guy smiled again.

"My dear mother, my life seems particularly clear and bright just now. What are these awful quagmires in my way?"

"Something upset and troubled you yesterday, when you went there to tea. I am certain something happened which made you unhappy. You cannot deceive your mother, Guy. I saw it in your face when you came home."

For some moments Guy was silent, and did not answer. When he spoke, the change in his voice startled her.

"Mother," he said, "it was no trivial trouble of my own last night, but the knowledge of the terrible sorrows of another; grief so bitter, that any little trials I have ever had appear utterly insignificant in comparison."

His voice shook with suppressed emotion.

"She has no right to tell you her troubles —troubles which, no doubt, are of her own making," said Guy's mother sharply. "She has no business to make a confidant of you."

Guy raised his head.

"And why not?" he asked quietly.

Either the reasons were so numerous that Mrs. Mervyn could not select one at a moment's notice, or they were too intangible to be put into words. Anyway, she contented herself with saying:

"I do wish you would forget both her and her troubles, and put them quite out of your mind."

Guy rose, and going to the window, leaned far out to get a breath of the cool night air. At his mother's words there had arisen in his mind a vision of the old-fashioned garden, bright with flowers, the fountain, the water-lilies, and those sweet lips, pressed again and again to the little gold-brown curl in the locket, with passionate love and longing; and again he heard that sad voice whispering: "It is all that is left me of my baby-boy."

A silence fell between mother and son.

She had said her say. Guy did not wish to answer.

Presently he called down into the garden below :

" Cyril, is that you ?"

" Yes."

" What are you doing all by yourself out there ?"

" Nothing particular. Is your mother with you, Mervyn ?"

" Yes."

" Anyone else ?"

" No, we are alone."

" May I come up ? I want to speak to you."

" Certainly."

" Have you and Cyril quarrelled ?" asked Mrs. Mervyn, as Guy turned away from the window.

" Quarrelled ? No, mother. Why ?"

" I thought he seemed rather silent and unlike himself to-day."

"Cyril has his troubles, like all the rest of the world, mother."

He stooped, and kissed her brow.

"You are not vexed with me, my son?"

"What a question, mother! Come in, old fellow. Draw up the arm-chair. It is getting almost too dark to see one another at a distance."

"I wanted to tell you," began Cyril abruptly, after a moment's silence, "that I think I must say good-bye, and go."

"Go!" exclaimed Mrs. Mervyn and Guy together. "What do you mean?"

"Why," said Cyril, speaking hurriedly and with evident effort, "I think it is rather a farce my living here now. You are so generous and so awfully good to me, and I do not want you to think me ungrateful. But the fact is, I don't like being paid for work I do not do. And now Guy has given up the idea of going to Cambridge, he needs coaching no longer; and as he has settled down at home again, he does not want a travelling companion : so I think it is time I looked out for a tutorship somewhere else."

The words seemed harsh and abrupt, but his tone was full of deep feeling.

Guy got up, and put his hand on Cyril's shoulder. "Nonsense!" he said. "I could not do without my tutor, or mother without her chaplain, or Berry without her patient victim." Then in a low voice he added : "My dear old fellow, yesterday unnerved and upset you. Don't talk like this before my mother. We will have it out alone."

"You must not leave us, Cyril," said Mrs. Mervyn. "I am sure we cannot spare you. And as for not working, you are always working for us all. We have quite come to look upon you as one of the family."

"You are most kind to me," answered Cyril gratefully. Then he raised his face, white and haggard, to Guy's. "I cannot stop here," he said.

"There goes the dressing-gong!" cried Guy. "Come on, Cyril. We won't let him go till he gets a fat living, will we, mother? Come to my room, old fellow; you have been moping all day. I have hardly seen you to speak to, except at meals."

He laid a strong hand on his friend's shoulder, and drew him out of the room.

Half an hour later Guy met his mother as she came downstairs.

"Mother," he said, "Cyril is going to London to-morrow. He has set his heart on seeing some old friends, and trying to hear of something else to do. Don't try and dissuade him. He will be the better for the change; and he has promised me faithfully to return on Monday. Even if he should hear of anything, we can easily persuade him then to give it up, and stay on with us."

"What has upset him, Guy?"

"Nothing connected with any of us, mother. It is an old trouble about an old friend. The kindest thing is to leave him alone now, and let him go his own way for a bit."

"Very well, dear, you are best able to judge."

"But where is Cyril?" cried Berry, as they took their places at the table.

"He is not well," explained Guy. "He has had a bad headache all day. Mother will have some dinner sent up to his room."

"I was sure he was ill," remarked Gertrude. "I told Beryl so, and tried to persuade her to leave him alone. But Beryl has so little consideration for anyone. Poor dear Cyril! Will he be down again to-night?"

"No; he prefers remaining in his room."

"Why did he come home so long before you yesterday, Guy?"

"He went over the houses with Miss Bruce. When they had seen them all, I was not in that part of the garden, so apparently Cyril did not wait for me."

"What a sweet-looking girl that Miss Bruce is!" said Mrs. Mervyn. "What do you think of her, Guy?"

"She is quite as nice as she looks," he replied, "which is high praise."

"I wish she was not staying at The Towers, then we might ask her here for tennis or something. There is such a dearth of nice girls in this neighbourhood."

"Well, mother, there is no reason you should not ask her. I have no doubt Lady Elaine would be pleased to bring her, if you like to invite them both."

"Oh dear no!" cried Gertrude. "We can't have that Lady Elaine here. Why, those Monks are cut sooner or later by all the neighbourhood. The Flamingos never *think* of calling there now! I don't see why you should raise your eyebrows, Guy. Lady Flamingo is far more generally received all about than *your* Lady Elaine! For my part, I consider them most objectionable people."

"The Flamingos?" said Guy. "Certainly. I entirely agree with you."

"Now, be quiet, Gertrude," interposed Mrs. Mervyn; "I am not going to invite Lady Elaine here, so there is no occasion to speak so strongly."

"Hullo, Berry! Why, what is the matter, little woman?"

Berry's tears were falling into her soup. She jumped up and hid her face on Guy's shoulder.

"Oh, Guy! I had no idea Cyril was ill! I have plagued him so to-day; but I thought he was sulky, or cross about something. And now I shall not be able to say goodnight to him, or tell him I am sorry."

Berry wept copiously.

"Never mind, dear," Guy said kindly, though half laughing, and wiping up Berry's tears with his dinner napkin. "You meant it as discipline, all for his good, didn't you? You shall come upstairs with me after dinner and say good-night, and tell him so, if you like. So don't break your poor little heart over it."

Berry returned to her place quite consoled.

Gertrude looked shocked.

" Why, surely, Guy, you don't intend——"

" Nonsense !" said Guy decidedly. " I do intend ! A sight of Berry will do more to cheer Cyril than anything. Do shut up, Gerty. You caused the trouble, to begin with ; so the least you can do is to say no more now."

Gertrude murmured something about " improprieties," and looked at her mother. But Mrs. Mervyn ignored the appeal. It was not often she vetoed any decision of Guy's.

" How superior our English cooking is to what we used to get abroad," she said, and so the subject dropped.

Later in the evening, after he had taken

Berry for her penitential visit, and then persuaded Cyril to go to bed, Guy escaped from the drawing-room, while Gertrude was at the piano and his mother dozing, and went out into the moonlight. He only intended to stroll about the garden and listen to the nightingales; but somehow he found himself striding down the avenue, and then out along the silent roads.

Guy wanted quiet. He wanted to be alone. He wanted time to think. Ever since his mountain climb in Switzerland, he always fancied that he could think best when going for a long walk.

Certainly it was quiet enough to-night. The moonlight was brilliant. His long dark shadow went on noiselessly before him. Not a sound but his own footsteps broke the stillness, and he silenced them by walking on the grass. The little village was asleep. As he passed through it, he saw lights in a few of the upper windows; but most of the cottages were in complete silence and darkness. The people in those parts were early risers, and went early to bed. Guy soon passed the last house in the village, and got into the lanes beyond; sandy lanes, with high banks on each side. Then he struck into the white high-road again.

All was still and silent as the grave. One old white horse looked at him over a fence; but appeared moonstruck and uncanny, and would not move, even when Guy poked its thin ribs with a stick. All nature seemed spellbound by that great weird white moon, sailing along overhead, keeping watch o'er the sleeping world. It reminded him of the night in Switzerland when he and Cyril had their long talk. Poor old Cyril! Guy's heart was very sore for his friend to-night; the more so, as he felt conscious of having misjudged him. He had thought him cold and hard, and certainly yesterday looked upon Muriel as the chief sufferer. But to-night, alone with him in his room, he had seen Cyril utterly break down, and cry out, in anguish of heart, for the girl he had loved and lost. And yet—while writhing under the recollection of those sweetly bitter hours spent with her the day before, of her every word, and look, and tone; and, above all, the almost certainty that he might have her now for the asking—he was firm in his old resolve. "No, Guy, no!" he had said. "She failed me then. I could not trust her again, I could not ask her to be my wife; I would not marry her even if she wished it. Hers cannot have been true love for me, or it would not have failed at the first trial. Oh, Muriel, my darling, my darling!" Guy's heart ached for his friend, and he reproached himself for having helped to bring about their meeting yesterday.

Yesterday! Cyril, Muriel—all else, was forgotten, as his mind went back to yesterday. Had he dreamt about that garden, with the rose-arch and the fountain and the many coloured flowers? Had he dreamt about the locket, with the little golden curl; and that *she* sat there before him, talking in a low, sweet voice, with an undertone of bitter pain in it, telling him how she had been a mother once, and had had a little son of her own to love and play with; how she had knelt on the floor to kiss his little feet; and how he was dead, and had not died in her arms?

Guy bared his head to the cool night breeze.

"Did I dream it all?" he cried. "Am I dreaming now? Or is it true!" Then the great silence all around began to oppress him, the moonlight seemed to bewilder him; and he turned, and began to race home, even faster than he had come.

As he walked, it all came back to him, every word he had said to her, and she to him; the minutest little details of all that happened in the garden. He even remembered how comical one of the goldfish looked as it opened its mouth and snapped at a little bit of moss she dropped into the fountain. He had hardly noticed it then; but now he remembered its exact expression, and how disgusted it seemed as it turned and swam away.

Yes, it was all true about that little dead baby's hair—*her* baby. All that sorrow, and suffering, and bitter pain; it was all true. Then he remembered how she had put her hand into his, and looked up at him with those sweet, wistful eyes, asking for sympathy and comfort. And he knew that when he left that garden he had felt years older than when he entered it.

Perhaps Mrs. Mervyn was right in saying that Lady Elaine had no business to make a confidant of Guy.

He had reached a lane not far from the park gates of The Towers.

He stood still, and looked up into the deep purple overhead.

"O my Lord," he said, "comfort her, as only Thou canst comfort. Give her Thy peace, which is not such as the world giveth. Soothe her heart with Thy love, which passeth knowledge; and oh, by Thy grace, help me to help her, and comfort her, and care for her; trusting Thee to keep me from falling."

A clock in the far distance struck ten. Guy had not thought it was so late.

Just as he began to hasten on, the sound of wheels rapidly approaching broke the stillness. The next moment a brougham came in sight, drawn by a pair of greys. Suddenly there flashed across Guy's mind the recollection of what he had seen on the tablets. *To ball at Lord K.'s with Monty.*

He stepped aside into the shadow, while they passed.

Just as the carriage was within a few yards

of where he stood, there was a shout; the coachman reined in the horses, so suddenly that they were almost thrown back upon their haunches. They drew up exactly opposite where Guy was standing. The footman sprang off the box and went to the open window. Guy could see the gleam of white and gold. He knew she was there—within three yards of him.

"James!" It was Lord Montague's loud, imperious voice. "Your mistress has forgotten her fan. We must go back for it."

"I beg your pardon, my lady," said the footman, "but I feel sure I saw it in your ladyship's hand just now."

She answered something; what, Guy could not hear.

"It does not seem to be here," said Lord Montague; "but it may have slipped down behind, somewhere."

He sprang out, and began searching in the bottom of the carriage.

"Oh, confound it!" he exclaimed impatiently. "With all this amount of white flue about, it is impossible to see if it is here or not."

Guy heard her laugh. She leaned forward to answer, and he caught every word.

"Don't make such a fuss, Monty. What does it matter? Surely I can go to a ball without a fan for once."

"It matters very much," he answered. "I have set my heart on your being seen with that fan to-night. There will not be another like it in the place. We will go back."

"I beg your pardon, my lord," said James again, deferentially; "but I am certain her ladyship had it when she entered the carriage."

"Suppose you get out, Elaine, and let the man look for it."

The footman took a dark rug off the box, and spread it on the road.

"Oh, bother, Monty!" she said impatiently; "what an absurd fuss you are making! Do get in and let us drive on."

But as Lord Montague still stood waiting by the carriage door, holding out his hand, she laughed in half amused vexation, and stepped out as he wished.

Then Guy saw her standing in the moonlight; such a vision of loveliness as made his heart beat, till he almost thought she must hear it.

"Now then!" said Lord Montague to the footman. "As you say it is there, shake out these wraps and rugs and find it."

Just as he turned to speak, Guy saw Lady Elaine, with a quick movement of her left hand, fling something white into the ditch. It almost touched his arm as it passed, and fell noiselessly into the long grass.

The cool night breeze stirred her golden hair. She coughed and shivered. Lord Montague drew her white plush wrap closer round her, and bent his dark, handsome head down very near to hers.

"Don't be vexed, dear," he said in a low tone. "I could not have that fan forgotten. All Kenneth's women-folk saw it, just after I bought it; and ever so many more in that set, who will be there to-night. They were green with envy; for there was not another like it to be had in London, for love or money. They were all dying to know who it was for. I would only tell them it was for one whom I considered 'peerless, queen among women.' They will know to-night; and when they have seen you, they will understand my having no eyes for any of them."

His dark face glowed as he spoke, and bent so near to hers, that a stray curl of her lovely hair blew against his cheek.

Guy, standing with clenched hands in the shadow, longed to escape, but could not do so unperceived.

Elaine turned away, half petulantly.

"Don't be foolish!" she said. "I had much sooner have no fan, than all this stupid fuss."

"How ungracious you are!" he murmured reproachfully. "Now I really believe, if that young hero of yours had given you a penny Japanese one, you would have taken more care of it!"

She laughed.

"Talk about what you understand, Monty. My young hero, as you call him, does not deal in fans and flattery. But now, really, I will stand here no longer."

"What a time the fellow is!" he exclaimed. "Now, then, have you found it?"

James had ascertained, at least two minutes before, that no fan was to be found. He turned ruefully from the search.

"I cannot see it, my lady."

"I thought so!" cried Lord Montague angrily. "You were an ass to say you had seen it at all, and cause all this delay! confound your stupidity! Get in, Elaine. We must drive back."

"I will not drive back!" she said decidedly. "If we return home, I shall stay there."

"Well, may I send this fellow back for it? He can ride after us."

"Do as you please," she answered coldly; "but do be good enough not to lose your temper."

"You hear?" said Lord Montague. "Walk back to The Towers as quickly as you can. It must have been left on the drawing-room table. I saw it there. Get it, and ride hard after us. You will overtake us, if you are quick. Look sharp!"

He sprang into the carriage after Lady Elaine. The coachman whipped up the horses. In a few moments they were out of sight. The footman muttered a few remarks, somewhat uncomplimentary to Lord Montague, and took his way back to The Towers.

Again all was silent and deserted, the

moonlight streaming on the bare white road.

Guy stepped out from the shadow.

"And she is going a ten-mile drive alone with that fellow, and ten miles back at some unearthly hour of the morning; and no one else with her at the ball!"

Guy stood looking down the road in the direction they had taken. Then the same queer sensation of dreaming came over him. It had all happened so quickly. Five minutes before he had been quite alone, and thinking of her—so differently. Had he really just seen her standing in her ball-dress, on this very spot?

Suddenly he remembered the white object she had flung away. He went to the ditch and soon found it; picked it up, and brought it into the moonlight. When he saw what it was he smiled grimly, and a kind of triumphant relief rose up in his heart.

An exquisite white fan; a lovely combination of delicately carved ivory and white feathers, mounted in gold.

Guy turned it over in his hand, opened and shut it once or twice; then flung it back into the ditch, and went his way.

CHAPTER XXV.

LONG before the time appointed in Guy's letter of invitation, little groups of the village people began to wend their way to Mervyn Park, and take their seats under the great oak, awaiting 'the young master' with no small amount of interest and curiosity.

It was a perfect Sabbath evening, calm, and still, and lovely. A settled peace seemed to rest upon all things. The people talked in low subdued voices, as they made their way across the park; and when they took their seats, waited silently as though the huge spreading branches overhead were consecrated rafters, listening to the evening songs of the birds, and watching the shy deer which peeped out at them from among the bracken.

"It's wonderful like Heaven here, this blessèd evening," whispered old Many Mussies to Beryl, who was settling her in a comfortable garden-chair, just opposite where Guy would stand. "Wonderful like Heaven, it seems to me. Ay, my dear, I can almost catch a sound o' the golden harps, behind the singing o' the birds. Bless the Lord! He sends us many, many mussies."

By Guy's special desire Mrs. Mervyn and the girls came out early, to see that all the old people had comfortable seats, where they would be able to hear nicely. He went off for a walk by himself as soon as tea was over.

Mrs. Mervyn received and welcomed the villagers as graciously as if they had been fashionable guests at a garden-party; and Gertrude and Beryl were assiduous in finding room for them all on the chairs and benches provided.

"There ain't no *let* seats 'ere!" said Tom the blacksmith, with a jovial grin of satisfaction, as he leaned back in the rustic arm-chair where Berry had just installed him, and folded his brawny arms across his chest. Tom was something of a democrat and socialist in his small way, and liked to scandalize his more conservative neighbours, whenever opportunity offered.

Ebenezer Bones, sitting near by, could not allow the remark to pass unanswered. He leaned forward till his heavy brass spectacles nearly slipped over the end of his nose, and said in a husky whisper:

"That's because there ain't no Quality."

"There's plenty o' quantity though!" rejoined Tom, who was somewhat of a wag; "a sight more'n what you get in that little chu'ch o' your'n. Look, they've got to sit around on the grass a'ready! Now when did you ever 'ave to make folks sit down in the h'ile ? eh ?"

Bones vouchsafed no reply ; but readjusted his glasses, took a peppermint lozenge, and opening his large black prayer-book, sat sternly erect, the personification of official and ecclesiastical dignity. Bones always took a peppermint lozenge when anything vexed him, and he wished to hold his tongue. Bones was " partial " to peppermint lozenges, and with one in his mouth silence became easy. Thanks to his wife, a bedridden old shrew, he got through a good many in the course of a week.

"And here comes the quality, too," went on Tom, in a lower tone ; " for I'm blest if this ain't her ladyship's self comin' along. I say, Muster Bones, bustle up and show her which is the chancel !"

A little giggling from kindred spirits near followed Tom's last remark ; but the old clerk made no reply, only drew in his cheeks spasmodically, and shook his head. Failing to get "a rise" out of him, Tom subsided.

Mrs. Mervyn tried to enter into a little friendly conversation with the old people; but they all appeared to consider themselves in church, and would only answer in rather shocked whispers; till presently old Betty Crow arrived upon the scene, apparently very much exhausted, and gasping for breath. Betty was what Guy called "an old caution." She had not been seen outside her own door for years. When she was safely seated, and had loosened her bonnet-strings, and ceased panting (which panting, by the way, only commenced when she got within hearing), Mrs. Mervyn came to her and said kindly :

"It is very nice to see you out, Mrs. Crow."

"Eh?"

Old Betty was very deaf indeed, unless

the question happened to be whether she could find any use for a half-crown.

Mrs. Mervyn tried the other ear. "It is very nice to see you out, Mrs. Crow."

"Eh?"

Mrs. Mervyn repeated her remark, in a tone of melancholy despair which somewhat belied the words.

"It is very nice to see you out, Mrs. Crow."

"No, I ain't nicely at all!" said old Betty, in a voice loud enough to be heard by all present. "I'm pertic'ler bad, *I* am! I've wonderful queer feels in m' inside. Nobody but God-a'-mighty knows what them queer feels o' mine is. Such a crawlin' and a creepin' and a poppin' and a thund'rin, as it's a mussy I ain't bust up altogether long afore this. Every blessèd night, when I goes to bed, I 'spects to find m'self in m' coffin by the mornin'. Nobody but the Lord as made me knows what awful experiences I do go through. It's all along o' me terrible bad indigester. No, I ain't nicely at all, thank ye, mum!"

Poor Mrs. Mervyn hurriedly returned to her seat, divided between feelings of horror and annoyance, and an irresistible desire to laugh. Lady Elaine had arrived just before the commencement of Betty's tirade, and was coughing behind her parasol.

At any other time Berry would have exploded, and gone off again during the rest of the evening whenever she looked at old Betty; but just now she felt positively ill with anxiety, and much too sick at heart to laugh at anything. Berry was so passionately proud of Guy, so desperately anxious that everyone should praise and admire him, and so fearful lest he should ever make a mistake, or do anything which people could criticise or laugh at. From the first she had not quite approved of this plan of his; it seemed such a formidable thing for Guy to stand up in public and speak to people. Surely, when he got here, every word he had meant to say would go out of his head, and he would stand there saying nothing, and everyone would wait in perfect silence. Berry nearly wept at the thought. It seemed like an awful nightmare. And Guy was anxious about it, too; she was quite sure of that, for he had only taken *one* cup of tea instead of three, and no cake at all, and then gone off for a walk by himself. Every fresh arrival added to Berry's miseries; and — oh, horror of horrors! here was Mr. Drawler, in his most clerical of best Sunday black coats, with his widest hat and stiffest dog-collar, and his sad-looking washed-out little wife on his arm.

"Oh, my blessed boy!" thought Berry, groaning inwardly, "if you should break down, how the Wicked Man will crow!"

And then in the distance she saw Guy coming, down from the woods and through the tall bracken. It became a positive necessity at that moment for Berry to unburden her mind to someone. Mr. Drawler was talking in his pompous way to her mother; Gertrude was occupied with Mrs. Drawler. Looking around for sympathy, Berry saw Lady Elaine sitting on a little low seat just behind the platform, close against the trunk of the tree. Evidently she, too, saw Guy coming, and was watching him, as he strode down the steep path and forced his way through the high bracken. Berry darted across, and said hurriedly in a low tone:

"Lady Elaine, I am so dreadfully afraid Guy will make a mess of it."

Elaine looked into the flushed, anxious little face.

"I am sure you needn't be afraid, dear," she said, with her sweetest smile. "He is certain to speak beautifully, and do us all good."

"Well, but here is this dreadful Mr. Drawler."

"Never mind. Guy will only be amused at his coming. You should have more confidence in Guy's rhetorical powers, Berry. Why, my dear child, you are trembling from head to foot! Sit down here by me. Whatever other people may think, you and I will agree with and admire every word he says—won't we? And look! here he is."

Guy found assembled a much larger audience than he had expected. Not only the respectable folk, in their Sunday best, but all the village ne'er-do-wells had brushed themselves up for once, and turned out in a body in response to his invitation; and having, much to their own satisfaction, arrived too late to find places on the seats, lounged about on the grass, looking half shy at being seen, half pleased with themselves for coming. And here is Mrs. Joram, carrying her prayer-book bound in crimson plush, with a large gold cross upon it. How complacently she is looking at—good gracious! Mr. Drawler! Guy's face fell. "I'll be bound she asked him to come!" he thought. He had seen from afar off that Lady Elaine was there; no doubt because a light dress is so quickly noticed from a distance, and she generally wore cream or white in summer.

As he came among them, all the people rose, with that old-fashioned courtesy so rarely met with now among the lower classes; the men pulled off their caps and the women dropped curtseys.

"Sit down, sit down, my friends!" said Guy, in his bright, cheery voice, as he made his way to where the gardeners had put him up a small platform.

Mr. Drawler came forward.

"Ah, how do you do, Sir Guy? Most gratifying—ah—to see so many of our flock —er—assembled in your park. Quite a delightful gathering. Eh? Yes, yes. *Just* so. And so highly favoured—er—by the weather; most highly favoured. *Quite* so. A perfectly charming evening. Now I—er—presume, Sir Guy, you would desire a chairman. If so, I am most happy to offer my services on this pleasant occasion."

"Oh, thanks," said Guy hurriedly; "but I don't think I shall want a chairman. I don't even call this a meeting. Nothing formal at all. I am only going to talk a little to our own people; just as simply as can be. I really only expected to find the villagers here; but it is very good of you to come, and very kind of you to offer, sir."

He passed on quickly, with a smile at his mother, and a nod to Mrs. Joram. As he mounted the platform, he saw Elaine on the low seat just behind him, and Berry seated on the grass, close beside her, with her two little brown hands clasped half-shyly, half-confidingly, round Elaine's arm. Guy's heart gave a great bound. "So she has won over

Berry at last!" he thought. He had been so afraid lest, if she came, she should be coldly received by his mother, and looked askance at by the girls, and made to feel unwelcome. But now Berry's whole attitude betokened that her warm, impulsive little heart was won; and Berry's love, once given, was given for ever.

Guy took this in at a glance, and rejoiced; but it all passed out of his mind the next moment, as he stood looking down at the crowd of people before him, all awakened into unusual interest and curiosity as to what he might have to say to them. Then he thought only of his Master and his message, as he noticed the careworn faces turned towards him, many of them deeply marked with lines of toil and weariness, telling of lives over-full of earthly cares and sorrows, and in which true joy, and the peace which is not such as the world giveth, had but little place.

Guy had anxiously and conscientiously prepared what he meant to say; but somehow he forgot it all now. He forgot the more critical portion of his audience behind him; he forgot that half an hour before he had come to the alarming conclusion that he had not the " gift of the gab"; he forgot the paper of closely written notes in his Bible; and leaning forward on the rail in front of him, he talked to the people assembled there as simply and naturally as if he were speaking to old Many Mussies over her cottage fire, instead of to an audience of two hundred and more.

Ah, and how they listened! Even the twittering of the birds seemed suddenly to cease, and a deep silence reigned around, broken only by that clear, earnest young voice, and the far distant tinkling of the sheep-bells in the valley.

And as he spoke he used, all unconsciously, that God-given gift of sympathy, and described the experience of tired souls who seek after rest, and find it not ; of weary hearts whom the world has disappointed—an experience which had not been his own, but which he read pictured forth in many of the faces before him, and dwelt upon with a touch so true and tender, that hearts long grown hard through trouble and disappointment softened into responsiveness, and tears ran down the careworn cheeks. And when he asked whether they did not feel the need of a friend to trust to, who could never change, who would never fail them—of some happiness which would last, and last for ever—a low " Ay, we do, sir !" broke from the men.

Then, with a ring of gladness in his voice—so infectious that the dull faces before him slowly brightened and lightened—Guy spoke of Jesus, *"the same yesterday, and to-day, and for ever ;"* of the Friend who faileth not, and changeth not. He told them just how it had dawned upon him that Jesus was willing and able to be something more to him than a mere God of doctrine, to be worshipped on Sundays, and forgotten all the week ; how he had sought Him, and found Him at last, a most mighty, precious Saviour.

The Gospel, simply and truly put, was news indeed to most of these people. They listened eagerly. Sunday after Sunday many of them had " sat under " Mr. Drawler in the little village church, where their fathers and forefathers had worshipped before them ; but never had his mild platitudes and scholarly expositions stirred their hearts like these simple earnest words from the young master. New possibilities seemed to open out before them. Some who had long resigned themselves to the idea that heaven could never be for them, got a little glimpse into the golden glory, and eagerly caught at the " whosoever cometh, I will in nowise cast out." And those who had long been secret, humble followers of the King felt their faith strengthen, and their hopes brighten, and their joy increase tenfold.

Only one amongst Guy's auditors listened with a sinking heart; and yet she was the one whom he most yearned to gladden. Why, as he grew brighter, did Lady Elaine feel more and more sad? She herself could hardly understand what caused the tightening, suffocating pain at her heart, which almost threatened to choke her. But, as she listened, sitting there with bent head at the foot of the old tree—as she heard "her boy" telling out of the fulness of his heart of this pure, perfect faith; of this holy heavenly joy which all might have; of this sweet love of Jesus, offered to all—her own heart cried out bitterly: "Not for me; oh, not for me!" And as Guy warmed to his subject, and his voice thrilled with love and gladness when he spoke of his dear Lord, the disappointment and aching at her heart increased. Why? Ah, why! It seemed such a little while ago that he cared for her opinion above all else; that he did her bidding in the smallest matters; ah, yes! that even his standard of right and wrong was her opinion. How well she remembered the look in his eyes, as he said: "If I saw *you* do something which I had always considered *wrong*, I should think it *right* from that moment!" And now his whole life was ruled by a power which had no place in hers.

But why should this make her heart ache?

Can it be only a year ago? Only a year since he was saying, with passionate tenderness, "I love you, sweet"—since his hot young kisses were on her lips, his strong young arms around her? Has she ever lost the feeling of either? And yet, now, it seems a wrong to him to remember that evening in the woods, which he so bitterly regrets. *Then* she indignantly said, "Go!" What would she say *now*, if it were to come over again?

She raises her beautiful head and looks at him. The slanting rays of the setting sun are shining on his bright brown hair. She cannot see his face; but somehow he looks to her, standing there in the sunlight, like some young god of ancient mythology descended to bring love and sunshine among mortals. Looking past him, she meets Mrs. Joram's eye: every little curl on each side of her kind old face is nodding approval; she tries in dumb-show to telegraph something across to her. Elaine feels morally certain it is, "*So* like St. Augustine, my dear;" but she has not the smallest inclination to laugh, or even to smile, just now.

"My friends," Guy is saying earnestly, "all this has to make a change in our lives.

We must not think we can make sure of heaven and then live just as we please down here. If a young man"—turning a little towards the rough specimens lounging on the grass around—"if a young man gives himself to Christ, it changes the whole purpose of his life; instead of living for himself, he now lives for his King. His servants *must* serve Him; but then what we say in church every Sunday is quite true: 'His service is perfect freedom.' I have tried it for a year, and I can tell you living for Him makes life worth living. But old things must pass away, old sins must be given up, if we are to be made really new men in Him. But, thank God! He not only forgives our past sins and puts them away for ever, but He also gives us the power to overcome present sin. Thank God, we can say day by day, 'through Him'—always through Him—'we are more than conquerors.' And so the old life passes away, and the new begins, and is lived, each day, for His glory."

Elaine's head drooped again.

"Yes; it is even so with him," she thought. "Old things *have* passed away. Years may come and years may go, but my boy-lover will come back to me—never!"

The sun went down in golden glory behind the purple hills.

"One word more, and I have done," Guy said. "Listen! I have urged you to trust yourselves to Jesus now—this very day—and receive His loving pardon. Don't put off coming to Him even till to-morrow. Why? You say you don't feel much like dying to-night—there is plenty of time before you. Well, suppose that to be so; before to-morrow morning dawns something else may have happened, which has nothing to do with how you feel to-night. Jesus Himself may be here. My friends, He is coming, coming soon! We know not when; but we watch and wait and expect Him very soon; for 'in such an hour as ye think not, your Lord doth come.' Even now, out of the crimson and gold of that sunset, we might see our King coming unto us."

Involuntarily they turned and followed the direction of his outstretched arm, looking with awe-struck, dazzled eyes at the golden glory over the hills. When they turned towards him again, Sir Guy was resting both arms on the rail, and leaning forward, he spoke his last words in low, earnest, pleading tones, which none present ever forgot.

"My friends, to-night Jesus says to every one of you, 'Come unto Me.' The invitation is quite free, and depends on nothing you have done or can do, only on His free love. But if you put off coming until you have to meet Him face to face as your Judge, then He will have to say to you, 'Depart.' The time for coming will be over; it will be too late. Oh, for God's sake, to-night—while His blessed 'Come' is ringing in your ears —come unto Him, and He will give you rest!"

END OF VOL. II.

BILLING AND SONS, PRINTERS, GUILDFORD.

www.ingramcontent.com/pod-product-compliance
Lightning Source LLC
Chambersburg PA
CBHW031737230426
43669CB00007B/381